Mastering the
Essay

EXERCISE WORKBOOK
AP* World History Edition

by Tony Maccarella

SHERPALEARNING
GUIDING YOU TO EVEN GREATER HEIGHTS

Sherpa Learning is dedicated to helping high-achieving learners gain access to high-quality, skills-based instruction that is created, reviewed, and tested by teachers. To learn more about Sherpa Learning and our vision, or to learn about some of our upcoming projects, please visit us at **www.sherpalearning.com**.

The publisher would like to thank Catherine Holden and Barbara Coutant for their contributions to the development of this text.

Publisher/Editor: David Nazarian

Copy-Editor: Christine DeFranco

Cartographer: Sal Esposito

Cover Design: Nazarian/Maccarella

Cover Image: View of Mt Fuji from Chureito Pagoda,
© Ryusakimaou/Dreamstime.com

* AP is a registered trademark of the College Board, which was not involved in the production of, and does not endorse, this product.

ISBN 978-0-9905471-8-1

SHERPALEARNING
GUIDING YOU TO EVEN GREATER HEIGHTS

Printed in the United States of America.

10 9 8 7 6 5 4 3 2 1

Table of Contents

How to Use this Book

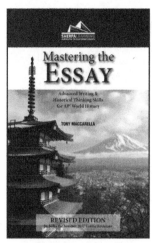

INSTRUCTIONAL HANDBOOK
ISBN: 978-0-9905471-6-7

Building on the Instructional Handbook

Each set of exercises in Part 1 of this Exercise Workbook is connected to a Guided Practice activity in the Instructional Handbook. As such, each Guided Practice can serve as a model for the exercises found in this workbook. Be sure to study each Guided Practice activity before beginning the corresponding set of exercises.

Chronological Periods

Because most World history teachers deliver their courses chronologically, each set of exercises in Part 1 of this workbook contains skills-based items organized into ascending chronological eras. This organization will help you to apply the information you are learning in school to each of the writing-skills exercises.

The number of items per historical period is roughly based upon the percentages of coverage on the exam, as defined by The College Board®.

Updated Content and Additional Resources

As changes are made to the AP World History curriculum, we will continually update the components of *Mastering the Essay* to align with those changes. Also, we will continue to develop new resources and activities to compliment or extend the activities found in *Mastering the Essay*.

All updates and new resources will be available to view or download through the *Mastering the Essay* page on the Sherpa Learning website. You'll also find a registration form so that we can notify you of new and updated materials.

www.sherpalearning.com/mte

 Or just scan this with your phone's camera to go directly to the site!

Part 1
Practice Exercises

Brainstorming and Organizing Evidence

For each of the following exercises, write down as many bits of specific evidence that you think might be relevant to the terms of the question. Do not try to answer the question in your mind yet—just brainstorm terms to generate a "picture" of your knowledge of the topic.

Once the evidence is in front of you, begin to group these bits into categories that could be applied to the tasks and terms of your question. Ask yourself these questions: *How are these terms connected to each other? How might this evidence help to illustrate those connections?* The questions you pose will suggest categories—themes, concepts, and characteristics—that help to demonstrate your understanding of the terms. Ultimately, the categories you create should help to explain HOW and/or WHY your evidence addresses the tasks and terms of the question.

Directions: Read the question and identify the tasks and terms. Then, brainstorm and organize the evidence you can remember into categories that help illustrate the connections among the tasks and terms.

1. THE NEOLITHIC REVOLUTION

Exercise Question: *Analyze the extent to which the Neolithic Revolution served as a cause for the establishment of civilizations.*

2. HORTICULTURE TO AGRICULTURE

Exercise Question: Analyze the extent to which the transition from horticulture to agriculture caused transformations in human organizations, gender roles, and culture.

3. UNIVERSAL RELIGIONS IN THE CLASSICAL PERIOD

Exercise Question: Analyze the reasons for the rapid expansion of universal religions across Eurasia in the classical period (600 BCE–600 CE).

4. GROWTH OF TRADING CITIES

Exercise Question: Compare and contrast the reasons for the growth of trading cities in different parts of the world from 600 CE to 1450 CE.

5. ISLAMIC KINGDOMS

Exercise Question: Compare and contrast the key characteristics of the two primary Islamic kingdoms of the 16th century, the Ottomans and the Safavids.

6. INDUSTRIALIZATION OF JAPAN AND BRITAIN

Exercise Question: Compare and contrast the process of industrialization in Japan with the earlier industrialization of Britain.

7. INTERWAR ART

Exercise Question: *To what extent was Interwar Art unique from art of the period immediately before World War I?*

8. WWII CONFERENCES AND COLD WAR POLICY

Exercise Question: *Analyze the impact of WWII Allied conferences on subsequent Cold War policy.*

2

Using the 3-Step Process to Analyze Documents for the DBQ

Directions: Identify the tasks and terms in each of the following questions, and then use the 3-Step Process to determine how each document might address those tasks and terms. Write your notes in the margins or on a separate piece of paper. As you analyze the documents, make a list of other specific evidence that comes to mind.

1. JEWISH DIASPORA IN THE CLASSICAL PERIOD

Exercise Question: In what ways did the Jewish diaspora of the classical period impact the bond amongst the followers of Judaism?

Document A

SOURCE: **Moses' Ten Commandments, Old Testament – Book of Exodus, Recorded in 6th Century BCE**

1) I am the Lord thy god, who brought thee out of the land of Egypt, out of the house of bondage.
2) Thou shalt have no other gods before Me.
3) Thou shalt not take the name of the Lord thy God in vain.
4) Remember the Sabbath day to keep it holy.
5) Honor thy father and thy mother.
6) Thou shalt not murder.
7) Thou shalt not commit adultery.
8) Thou shalt not steal.
9) Thou shalt not bear false witness against thy neighbor.
10) Thou shalt not covet anything that belongs to thy neighbor.

Document B

> **Source: Jeremiah, Jewish Prophet, Old Testament – Book of Kings, 6th Century BCE**
>
> Then the king of Assyria sent the Tartan, the Rabsaris, and the Rabshakeh from Lachish, with a great army against Jerusalem, to King Hezekiah. And they went up and came to Jerusalem. When they had come up, they went and stood by the aqueduct from the upper pool, which was on the highway to the Fuller's Field. And when they had called to the king, Eliakim the son of Hilkiah, who was over the household, Shebna the scribe, and Joah the son of Asaph, the recorder, came out to them. Then the Rabshakeh said to them, "Say now to Hezekiah, 'Thus says the great king, the king of Assyria: "What confidence is this in which you trust? You speak of having plans and power for war; but they are mere words. And in whom do you trust, that you rebel against me?"

Document C

> **Source: Sanhedrin 17B, Laws by a Court of Judges in Jewish cities, c. 50 BCE**
>
> A *talmid hakham* (Torah scholar) is not allowed to live in a city that does not have these 10 things: a *beit din* (law court) that metes out punishments; a *tzedakah* (charity) fund that is collected by two people and distributed by three; a synagogue; a bath house; a bathroom; a doctor; a craftsperson; a blood-letter; and a teacher of children.

Document D

SOURCE: **Josephus, Judeo-Roman Historian, *The Wars of the Jews –* *Book 6*, commissioned by the Roman emperor, Vespasian, 1ˢᵗ Century CE**

So the Romans being now become masters of the walls, they both placed their ensigns upon the towers, and made joyful acclamations for the victory they had gained, as having found the end of this war much lighter than its beginning; for when they had gotten upon the last wall, without any bloodshed, they could hardly believe what they found to be true; but seeing nobody to oppose them, they stood in doubt what such an unusual solitude could mean. But when they went in numbers into the lanes of the city, with their swords drawn, they slew those whom they overtook, without mercy, and set fire to the houses wither the Jews were fled, and burnt every soul in them, and laid waste a great many of the rest; and when they were come to the houses to plunder them, they found in them entire families of dead men, and the upper rooms full of dead corpses, that is of such as died by the famine; they then stood in a horror at this sight, and went out without touching anything.

Document E

SOURCE: **Relief of the Siege of Jerusalem on the Arch of Titus, Rome, Italy, 1ˢᵗ Century CE**

Document F

SOURCE: Greek Inscription on a Synagogue, Jerusalem, 1st Century CE

Theodotos, son of Vettenus, priest and ruler of the synagogue, son of
a ruler of the synagogue, grandson of a ruler of the synagogue, built
the synagogue for the reading of the Torah and the teaching of the
commandments, and also the guest chamber and the upper rooms and
the ritual pools of water for lodging for those needing them from abroad,
which his fathers, the elders and Simonides founded.

Document G

SOURCE: Map of Jewish Diaspora from 4th Century BCE to
2nd Century CE

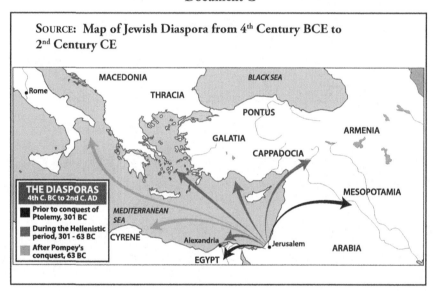

---

2. EFFECTS OF THE WEST AFRICAN KINGDOMS

Exercise Question: Analyze the cross-cultural effects of
trade with the Western African Kingdoms in the Medieval Period
(900 CE–1550 CE).

Document A

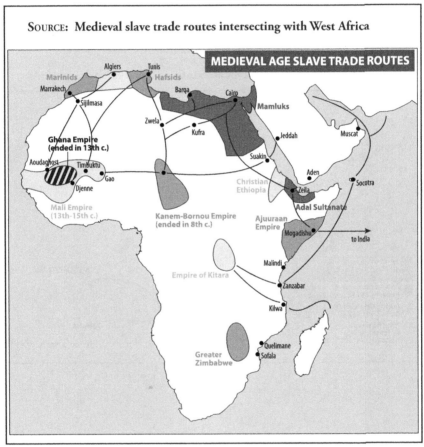

SOURCE: **Medieval slave trade routes intersecting with West Africa**

Document B

SOURCE: **Joannes Leo Africanus (c. 1494–c. 1554), a Spanish Muslim and author of "Description of Africa," c. 1526**

In the center of the city [Timbuktu] is a temple built of stone and mortar, built by an architect named Granata, and in addition there is a large palace, constructed by the same architect, where the king lives. The shops of the artisans, the merchants, and especially weavers of cotton cloth are very numerous. Fabrics are also imported from Europe to Timbuktu, borne by Berber merchants... The inhabitants are very rich, especially the strangers who have settled in the country; so much so that the current king has given two of his daughters in marriage to two brothers, both businessmen, on account of their wealth ... Grain and animals are abundant, so that the consumption of milk and butter is considerable. But salt is in very short supply because it is carried here from Tegaza, some 500 miles from Timbuktu. I happened to be in this city at a time when a load of salt sold for eighty ducats. The king has a rich treasure of coins and gold ingots. One of these ingots weighs 970 pounds.

Document C

SOURCE: **Ibn Battuta, a Muslim traveler, in the "Rihla," a published personal record of his trip, written three years after his return, 1535**

The sultan comes out of a door in a corner of the palace, carrying a bow in his hand and a quiver on his back. On his head he has a golden skull-cap, bound with a gold band which has narrow ends shaped like knives, more than a span in length. His usual dress is a velvety red tunic, made of the European fabrics called "mutanfas." The sultan is preceded by his musicians, who carry gold and silver guimbris [two-stringed guitars], and behind him come three hundred armed slaves...

... The negroes [in Mali] possess some admirable qualities. They are seldom unjust, and have a greater abhorrence of injustice than any other people. Their sultan shows no mercy to anyone who is guilty of the least act of it. There is complete security in their country. Neither traveler nor inhabitant in it has anything to fear from robbers or men of violence.... They are careful to observe the hours of prayer, and assiduous in attending them in congregations, and in bringing up their children to them.

Document D

SOURCE: **Catalan Atlas, Spanish Map, produced by the Majorcan Cartographic School, 1375**

Document E

> **SOURCE: Al-Bakir, a Spanish Muslim, personal account, c. 11th century**
>
> The king [of Ghana] exacts the right of one dinar of gold on each donkey-load of salt that enters his country, and two dinars of gold on each load of salt that goes out. A load of copper carries a duty of five mitqals and a load of merchandise ten mitqals. The best gold in the country comes from Ghiaru, a town situated eighteen days' journey from the capital [Kumbi] in a country that is densely populated by Negroes and covered with villages. All pieces of native gold found in the mines of the empire belong to the sovereign, although he lets the public have the gold dust that everybody knows about; without this precaution, gold would become so abundant as practically to lose its value.... The Negroes ... known as Nougharmarta are traders, and carry gold dust from Iresni all over the place....

Document F

> **SOURCE: Arabic Manuscripts on astronomy and mathematics from Timbuktu, Medieval Period**
>
>

Document G

SOURCE: **Alvise da Cadamosto, Italian Slave Trader and Explorer sailing for Portugal, "Description of Capo Bianco and the Islands Nearest to It," c. 1475**

You should also know that behind this Capo Bianco on the land, is a place called Hoden, which is about six days inland by camel. This place is not walled, but is frequented by Arabs, and is a market where the caravans arrive from Tanbutu [Timbuktu]… They are Muhammadans, and very hostile to Christians….They are very numerous, and have many camels on which they carry brass and silver from Barbary and other things to Tanbuto and to the land of the Blacks. Thence they carry away gold and pepper, which they bring hither….

You should know that the said Lord Infante of Portugal [the crown prince, Henry the Navigator] has leased this island of Argin to Christians [for ten years], so that no one can enter the bay to trade with the Arabs save those who hold the license. These have dwellings on the island and factories where they buy and sell with the said Arabs who come to the coast to trade for merchandise of various kinds, such as woollen cloths, cotton, silver, and "alchezeli," that is, cloaks, carpets, and similar articles and above all, corn, for they are always short of food. They give in exchange slaves whom the Arabs bring from the land of the Blacks, and gold tiber.

3. EXPANSION OF LANDED EMPIRES

Exercise Question: Analyze the causes of the expansion of landed empires from 1450 to 1750.

Document A

SOURCE: Godfrey Kneller, lead British portrait painter, "Portrait of Peter the Great of Russia," 1698

Document B

SOURCE: Alexander Gordon, Russian General under Peter the Great, *The History of Peter the Great,* **1718**

In the year 1703 the tsar took the field early, cantoned his troops in the month of March, and about the 20th of April brought the army together; then marched and invested another small but important place called Neva-Chance, which surrendered on the 14th of May. The commodious situation of this place made the tsar resolve to erect on it a considerable town, with a strong citadel, consisting of six royal bastions, together with good outworks; this he soon put into execution and called it St. Petersburg, which is now esteemed so strong that it will be scarcely possible for the Swedes ever to take it by force...

The foundation was thus laid: trees of about thirty feet in length and about fifteen inches thick were taken and joined artfully together into chests ten feet high; these chests were filled with stones of great weight, which sunk down through the sea, and made a very solid foundation, upon which he raised his fort, called Kronstadt.

Document C

SOURCE: **Francois Bernier, a French physician and traveler attached to the Mughal court for 12 years, "An Account of India and the Great Moghul," 1655**

My lord, you may have seen before this, by the maps of Asia, how great every way is the extent of the empire of the Great Mogul, which is commonly called India or Indostan. I have not measured it mathematically; but to speak of it according to the ordinary journeys of the country...that it is at least five times as far as from Paris to Lyons...

[M]ore than an hundred rajahs, or considerable heathen sovereigns, dispersed through the whole empire, some near to, others remote...The Mogul is obliged to keep these rajahs in his service for sundry reasons: the first, because the militia of the rajahs is very good (as was said above) and because there are rajahs (as was intimated also) any one of whom can bring into the field above twenty-five thousand men; the second, the better to bridle the other rajahs and to reduce them to reason, when they cantonize, or when they refuse to pay tribute, or when, out of fear or other cause, they will not leave their country to serve in the army when the Mogul requires it; the third, the better to nourish jealousies and keenness among them, by favoring and caressing one more than the other, which is done to that degree that they proceed to fight with one another very frequently.

Document D

SOURCE: **Ogier Ghiselin de Busbecq, Dutch Ambassador to the Ottoman Empire,** *The Turkish Letters*, **1555–1562**

At Buda [the western portion of modern-day Budapest] I made my first acquaintance with the Janissaries; this is the name by which the Turks call the infantry of the royal guard. The Turkish state has 12,000 of these troops when the corps is at its full strength. They are scattered through every part of the empire, either to garrison the forts against the enemy, or to protect the Christians and Jews from the violence of the mob. There is no district with any considerable amount of population, no borough or city, which has not a detachment of Janissaries to protect...A garrison of Janissaries is always stationed in the citadel of Buda...

The Turkish monarch going to war takes with him over 400 camels and nearly as many baggage mules, of which a great part are loaded with rice and other kinds of grain. These mules and camels also serve to carry tents and armour, and likewise tools and munitions for the campaign...On their side is the vast wealth of their empire, unimpaired resources, experience and practice in arms, a veteran soldiery, an uninterrupted series of victories, readiness to endure hardships, union, order, discipline, thrift and watchfulness...No distinction is attached to birth among the Turks; the deference to be paid to a man is measured by the position he holds in the public service. There is no fighting for precedence; a man's place is marked out by the duties he discharges...[H]e considers each case on its own merits, and examines carefully into the character, ability, and disposition of the man whose promotion is in question.

Document E

SOURCE: **Fathers Simon and Vincent, report to the Pope on the Safavid Ruler – Shah Abbas I, c. 1621**

The king, Shah Abbas ... is [43] years old. ... He enrolled in the armed forces large numbers of Georgian, Curcassian, and other golams, and created the office of commander in chief...which had not previously existed under the Safavid regime. Several thousand men were drafted into regiments of musketeers... Into the regiment of musketeers, too, were drafted all the riff-fall from every province – sturdy, serviceable men who were unemployed and preyed on the lower class...

As regards to his knowledge of the outside world, he possesses information about the rulers (both Muslim and non-Muslim) of other countries, about the size and composition of their armies, about their religious faith and the organization of their kingdoms, about their highway systems, and about their prosperity.

Document F

SOURCE: "Shah Jahan on Horseback," Mughal Emperor, painted by the court painter Payag, c. 1633

Document G

SOURCE: Articles of Agreement between Cossacks and Russian Tsar, 1654

In the beginning, grant that Your Tsarist Majesty will confirm our rights and our military freedoms as they have existed for ages…; grant that neither a military commander nor a boyar nor court official shall interfere with the courts of the Army and that its members be judged by their own elders. …That the Zaporozhian [Cossack] Army to the number of sixty thousand men always be at full strength…

That the Zaporozhian [Cossack] Army on its own select from within itself a hetman (or commander) and make him known to His Tsarist Majesty…

That no one take away Cossack properties,

That to the general secretary of the Zaporozhian [Cossack] Army there be allocated, because of the kindness of His Tsarist Majesty, one thousand gold pieces for the employees of his office and a mill to provide for quartermaster needs.

That to each colonel there be assigned a mill because expenditures are great.

That envoys from foreign lands coming to the Zaporozhian [Cossack] Army with good intentions be freely received by the Lord Hetman and the Zaporozhian Army.

That His Tsarist Majesty write down our privileges in charters stamped by seals, one for Cossack freedoms and a second for the freedoms of the gentry, so that these freedoms might be forever. And when we shall receive this, we ourselves are to maintain order among ourselves. He who is a Cossack shall have Cossack freedoms, and he who is a land-working peasant shall give to His Tsarist Majesty the customary obligation, as before.

4. STABILITY OF THE MUGHAL EMPIRE

Exercise Question: *Analyze the stability of the Mughal Empire between 1504 and 1858.*

Document A

SOURCE: **Zahir-u-din Muhammad Babur, from *The Babur-nama* (*Book of Babur*), an autobiography of the first Mughal ruler, Babur, c. 1529**

(24 December) We crossed the Bihat River at a ford below the Jhelum River and dismounted there.

(25 December) Sayyid Tufan and Sayyid Lachin were sent galloping off, each with a pair of horses, to say in Lahore, 'Do not join battle; meet us at Sialkot or Pasrur.' It was in everyone's mouth that Apaq Ghazi Khan had collected 30,000 to 40,000 men, and that Daulat Khan, old as he was, had girt two swords to his waist, and that they were both resolved to fight. I thought, 'The proverb says that ten friends are better than nine. Do not make a mistake. When the Lahore begs [chiefs] have joined you, fight there and then!'

Document B

SOURCE: **Farhat Hasan, Professor of History, University of Delhi, from** *State and Locality in Mughal India: Power Relations in Western India, C. 1572–1730,* **2006**

Perhaps, no city or town in Mughal India was without a *kotwal.* He was responsible for the safety and protection of the people living in a city or town. He would hunt down thieves, punish criminals, imprison delinquents and keep a record of all people living in the various quarters of the town (*muhalla*). He was also some kind of censor of morals, preventing people from visiting brothels and taverns. Described as 'the governor of the night', his severity and capriciousness attracted much attention of European travelers. His services were not free, and for ensuring protection to the inhabitants of the town, he had his officials from among the local service gentry to assess and realize a 'protection cess [tax]' from the dwellers and shopkeepers. These cesses were known as *rusum-I kotwali*. In addition, he took money from offenders and criminals as fines or *jurmana*. The other important taxes that he realized included road tolls (*rahdari*), *tarazu kasha* (a tax on stamping weights and measures) and *chhati* (a cess per cartload). The cesses collected in the *kotwali* constituted a separate fiscal unit in Surat and Cambay, which was called, *mahal-I chabutra-I kotwali*.

Document C

SOURCE: **Salma Ahmed Farooqui, Associate Professor of History at the Directorate of Distance Education, Maulana Azad National Urdu University, Hyderabad, from** *A Comprehensive History of Medieval India: Twelfth to the Mid-Eighteenth Century,* **2011**

Humayan's son and successor, Akbar, was born to queen Hamida Banu Begum, the daughter of a cultured Shia family. By personal conviction, however, Akbar was a Sunni. He was brought up in a cosmopolitan atmosphere and was broad minded by nature. He, therefore, displayed the spirit of toleration and harmony in all his actions and decisions. When Akbar assumed power, he found that the participation of the regional political elite in running the affairs of the state was not only essential to overcome certain hurdles, but also important for the healthy existence of the state. Therefore, Akbar had to choose between the Islamic orthodoxy and the more fruitful Indianization of his political regime.

Under the influence of his regent, tutors and friends, Akbar's religious views underwent great change with the passage of time. He was inquisitive by nature and wanted to learn the true essence behind every religion; he never condemned any religion by word or deed. In 1562 CE, Akbar married the daughter of Raja Bharmal of Amber – a matrimonial alliance which marked the beginning of his new religious policy aimed at appeasing the Rajputs and other non-Muslim groups. The marriage helped to end the age-old friction between the Rajputs and the Muslims in India. In 1563 CE, Akbar abolished the pilgrimage tax which was levied on Hindus during their pilgrimages; and the very next year (1564 CE) he abolished the *jiziya,* or the poll tax, which was levied on all non-Muslims. He also removed the restrictions imposed on the construction of places of worship by non-Muslims. As a result, new temples and churches came up in various parts of the empire.

Document D

SOURCE: **John F. Richards, Professor of History, Duke University, North Carolina, from** *The Mughal Empire*, **1995**

Within the formal boundaries of the empire, tightening and deepening imperial domination resumed. For Jahangir, the most irksome internal problem was that of the Rana of Mewer [Amar Singh], head of the Sisodia clan of Rajputs at Udaipur who had successfully defied Akbar.... Equipping his son Prince Khurram with a new army the emperor sent him into the hills of Rajasthan. Khurram set up a series of military checkpoints in the hills at points thought inaccessible by Mughal commanders; sent one after the other columns of cavalry to harry the Rana and his commanders; and made hostages of the families of the most prominent Sisodias. Finally, unable to discourage the grimly determined Mughal prince, Amar Singh capitulated.

The Rana "chose obedience and loyalty" .... Amar Singh presented himself in person to Khurram and formally submitted. Pleading old age, he asked that his son and heir Karan travel to Jahangir's court and be enrolled as an imperial amir in his place. Delighted by this victory, Jahangir agreed and Khurram returned to a great celebration in Ajmer....

The capitulation of the Rana of Mewer signaled that resistance to the Mughal was futile. No mountainous or desert refuge was safe. Proud Rajas such as the Jam of Kathiawar, the remote peninsula in Gujarat, who had never appeared in person at the court of the Sultans of Gujarat or of Akbar, prudently decided to prostrate themselves before Jahangir....

In hundreds of localities rajas or lineage heads who had experienced only sporadic encounters with Indo-Muslim rulers now found themselves faced by forcible demands for ritual submission and payment of annual tribute.

Document E

SOURCE: **On behalf of Emperor Aurangzeb, Mughal ruler, General Order for the Destruction of Temples, issued 9 April 1669**

The Lord Cherisher of the Faith learnt that in the provinces of Thatta, Multan and especially at Benaras, the Brahmin misbelievers used to teach their false books in their established schools, and their admirers and students, both Hindu and Muslim, used to come from great distances to these misguided men in order to acquire their vile learning. His Majesty, eager to establish Islam, issued orders to the governors of all the provinces to demolish the schools and temples of the infidels, and, with the utmost urgency, put down the teaching and the public practice of the religion of these unbelievers...

Document F

SOURCE: **On behalf of Emperor Aurangzeb, Mughal ruler, Reimposition of Jizyah, issued 2 April 1679**

As all the aims of the religious Emperor were directed to the spreading of the law of Islam and the overthrow of the practices of the infidels, he issued orders to the high diwani officers that from Wednesday, the 1st Rabi I (2nd April 1679), in obedience to the Quranic injunction, "till they pay commutation money (Jizyah) with the hand in humility", and in agreement with the canonical tradition, Jizyah should be collected from the infidels (zimmis) of the capital and the provinces. Many of the honest scholars of the time were appointed to discharge the work (of collecting Jizyah). May god actuate him (Emperor Aurangzeb) to do that which He loves and is pleased with, and make his future life better than the present.

Document G

SOURCE: **Abu Fazl, official court historian and personal friend of Akbar, writing of the year 1562 in** *Akbar-nama: The History of Akbar*, **c. 1594**

One of the glorious boons of his Majesty the Shahinshah which shone forth in this auspicious year was the abolition of enslavement. The victorious troops which came into the wide territories of India used in their tyranny to make prisoners of the wives and children and other relatives of the people of India, and used to enjoy them or sell them. His Majesty the Shahinshah, out of his thorough recognition of and worship of God, and from his abundant foresight and right thinking gave orders that no soldier of the victorious armies should in any part of his dominions act in this manner. ... It was for excellent reasons that His Majesty gave his attention to this subject, although the binding, killing or striking the haughty and the chastising the stiff-necked are part of the struggle for empire – and this is a point about which both sound jurists and innovators are agreed – yet it is outside of the canons of justice to regard the chastisement of women and innocent children as the chastisement of the contumacious. If the husbands have taken the path of insolence, how is it the fault of the wives, and if the fathers have chosen the road of opposition what fault have the children committed?

5. NAPOLEON IN EGYPT

Exercise Question: Discuss the impact of Napoleon on the culture and society of Egypt.

Document A

SOURCE: **al-Jabarti, Egyptian historian and eyewitness to French occupation, speaking of the early 18th century, c. 1798**

Egypt was glowing with beauty during that time [before Napoleon] ... the poor had enough to eat, high and low alike lived comfortably.

Document B

SOURCE: **Napoleon Bonaparte, proclamation to the people of Egypt, 1798**

We, too, are true Mussulmans [Muslims]. Is it not we who have destroyed the Pope that said war must be made on the Mussulmans? Is it not we who have destroyed the Knights of Malta because those insensate chevaliers believed God wanted them to make war on the Mussulmans? Thrice happy they who are on our side! They shall prosper in their fortune and in their place. Happy those who are neutral! They shall have time to understand us, and shall array themselves with us. But woe, thrice woe, to those who shall take up arms for the Mamelukes and fight against us! There shall be no hope left for them; they shall perish.

Document C

SOURCE: **Napoleon Bonaparte, proclamation to the people of Egypt, 1798**

What wisdom, what talents, what virtues distinguish the Mamelukes, so that they have exclusive possession of everything that makes life sweet and enjoyable? Is there a fine piece of land? It belongs to the Mamelukes. Is there a beautiful slave girl, a fine horse, a handsome house? Those things too belong to the Mamelukes. If Egypt is their farm, let them show us the lease that God gave them on it!

Document D

SOURCE: **Louis Antoine Fauvelet de Bourrienne, writing of Napoleon's order to execute Mameluke rebels in 1798, in his memoirs, c. 1830**

The sacks were opened in the principal square, and the heads rolled out before the assembled populace. I cannot describe the horror I experienced: but at the same time, I must confess that it had the effect for a considerable time of securing tranquility.

Document E

SOURCE: **Louis Antoine Fauvelet de Bourrienne, Napoleon's secretary, in his memoirs, c. 1830**

Shortly before our departure I asked Bonaparte how long he intended to remain in Egypt. He replied, "A few months, or six years: all depends on circumstances. I will colonize the country. I will bring them artists and artisans of every description; women, actors, etc. We are but nine-and-twenty now, and we shall then be five-and-thirty."

Document F

SOURCE: **J.A. St. John, traveler to Egypt, in his memoirs, 1834**

Both in the army and fleet, schools are established, where the soldiers and sailors are taught reading, writing, and arithmetic. The rude fellah from the wilds of Gournu, taken away from the fields at the age of thirty, is now daily seen bending over his slate. No soldier unable to read and write can be promoted to the rank of corporal.

Document G

SOURCE: **Chancellor Pasquier, former member of the Parlement of Paris, commenting in his memoirs about Napoleon's reports from Egypt, date unknown**

What had especially struck people in these bulletins was a certain declaration in favour of the Mohammedan creed, the effect of which, though it might be somewhat great in Egypt, had in France only called forth ridicule.

6. ITALIAN IMMIGRATION TO ARGENTINA

Exercise Question: *Analyze the extent to which Italian immigration to Argentina in the late 19th and early 20th centuries was beneficial to both countries.*

Document A

SOURCE: from Argentina's National Constitution, 1853 (reinstated in 1983 and amended through 1994)

We, the representatives of the people of the Argentine Nation, assembled in General Constituent Congress by the will and election of the provinces which compose it, in fulfillment of pre-existing pacts, with the object of constituting the national union, ensuring justice, preserving domestic peace, providing for the common defense, promoting the general welfare, and securing the blessings of liberty to ourselves, to our posterity, and to all men in the world who wish to dwell on Argentine soil: invoking the protection of God, source of all reason and justice, do ordain, decree and establish this Constitution for the Argentine Nation.

Part 1

Chapter I: Declarations, Rights, and Guarantees

...

Article 23

The Federal Government shall encourage European immigration, and it may not restrict, limit, or burden with any tax whatsoever the entry into Argentine territory of foreigners whose purpose is tilling the soil, improving industries, and introducing and teaching the sciences and the arts.

Document B

SOURCE: **J. H. Senner, Commissioner of Immigration at the Port of New York, from "Immigration from Italy,"** *The North American Review*, 1896

The Italians only, of all the Latin peoples, developed a tendency to migration ... and until a very recent date such immigration into the United States was very much smaller than that into the southern part of the Western Continent, especially the Argentine Republic.... Poor Italy had suffered perpetually from misrule and bloody wars and consequent commercial depression. United Italy, only a little more than a quarter of a century in existence, could not as yet succeed in securing safety, peace, and welfare to her subjects ... refrained from opposing such emigration, and has even seemingly favored it.

For a good many years this policy of the Italian Government seemed to produce advantageous results to the prosperity of Italy. As long as the migration to and fro was entirely unrestricted, Italians in large numbers were in the habit of crossing and recrossing the ocean, some as many as ten times, as so-called "birds of passage," and taking out of the United States, or other countries of America, the gains which their standard of living, far below that of an American wage earner, made it easy for them to accumulate. The amount of money annually sent home by Italian laborers or taken back by them has been conservatively estimated at from $4,000,000 to even $30,000,000.... But these advantages to the old country are about to cease definitely. The rigid enforcement of the Federal statutes since 1893 by the United States Immigration Officials has made it very hard for Italian " birds of passage" to come and go at their pleasure. Besides, quite a large proportion of those who originally came to the United States with no intention of acquiring residence, found the country so advantageous and congenial to them that they changed their minds, sent for their families and settled permanently within the United States, acquiring, in time, rights of citizenship.

Document C

SOURCE: **Walter F. Willcox, an American statistician and pioneer of demography, from a collection of immigration statistics in Argentina, Brazil, Paraguay, Uruguay, Chile published in** *International Migrations, Volume I: Statistics,* **1929**

Table III—Distribution, by Occupation, of Immigrant Aliens (2nd & 3rd Class Passengers), by Sea (in Decades), 1857–1924

Year	Total	Agriculture	Industry and Mining	Transport and Commerce	Domestic Service and General Labor	Liberal Professions and Public Services	Other occupations, none, or unknown
1857-1860	20,000	9,421	1,105	823	1,850	124	6,677
1861-1870	159,570	77,671	4,699	4,053	16,373	554	56,220
1871-1880	260,885	100,701	18,319	8,653	24,780	2,064	106,368
1881-1890	841,122	454,919	67,686	26,217	93,115	5,288	193,897
1891-1900	648,326	288,429	50,613	29,068	127,415	4,364	148,437
1901-1910	1,764,103	562,884	161,092	107,983	493,685	14,248	424,211
1911-1920	1,204,919	211,061	99,858	75,289	449,196	16,789	352,726
1921-1924	582,351	142,838	71,187	48,888	125,120	11,854	181,864

Document D

SOURCE: Leonard Nakamura, economic researcher, Federal Reserve Bank of Philadelphia, from a working paper analyzing early-twentieth-century stock prices in Argentina, 1997

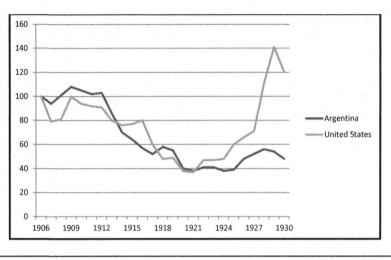

Document E

SOURCE: **Daniela Del Boca, Professor of Economics, University of Torino, from a discussion paper analyzing Italian emigration patterns, 2003**

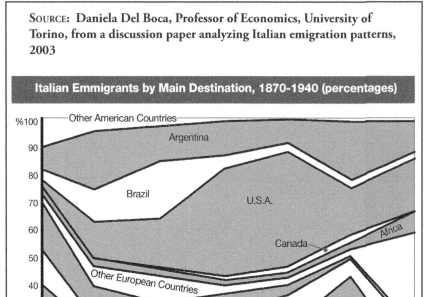

Italian Emmigrants by Main Destination, 1870-1940 (percentages)

Document F

SOURCE: from "Argentina – Overview of the History of International Migration in Argentina," a report summarizing immigration statistics for the history of Argentina, published by the Organization of American States, 2014

After obtaining its independence from Spain at the beginning of the 19th century, Argentina adopted an open immigration policy and encouraged immigrants to adopt the country as their own. For a brief period of time at the end of the 1880s, the government subsidized passage tickets for immigrants. It is estimated that the country received more than seven million immigrants between 1870 and 1930, mainly from Spain and Italy. The reasons for this mass exodus from Europe are several…. In the case of the Italian immigrants, Argentina promised to be a new opportunity as they left behind a country impoverished by the unification of the Italian states where unemployment, overpopulation, and serious political conflicts prevailed.

Massive immigrations from Europe responded in part to the offer of better wages. On average, a farm worker earned in four or five months of harvesting, between five and ten times more than what he/she earned in his/her country of origin. Another point of attraction was government programs. In 1862, [Argentina's] Congress authorized the hiring of immigrants to colonize national territories, specifically the regions external to the constituted provinces that were governed from Buenos Aires. The Office of Migration (Dirección de Migraciones), established in 1869, appointed agents in Europe to recruit colonists. The new arrivals enjoyed free accommodations, tax exemption on their possessions, and also, as time evolved, free rail transportation. Many of the first immigrants achieved quick social mobility; although very few were able to acquire lands.

In 1854, Buenos Aires had a population of 90,000 inhabitants; towards 1869, the population increased to 177,000, including 41,000 Italians and 20,000 Spaniards; in 1895, the number rose to 670,000. In 1914, the immigrant population represented 30% of the total population. In Buenos Aires, estimates of the immigrant population … vary between 60% and 80%….

Document G

SOURCE: **Jutta Bolt, Professor of Economics, Lund University, Netherlands, from "GDP per Capita since 1820," in** *How Was Life?: Global Well-being since 1820,* **2014**

GDP per Capita (USD)

Decade	Argentina	Italy
1820	998	1,511
1830	---	1,507
1840	---	1,537
1850	1,251	1,481
1860	1,355	1,459
1870	1,468	1,542
1880	1,604	1,589
1890	2,416	1,690
1900	2,875	1,855
1910	3,822	2,176
1920	3,473	2,153
1930	4,080	2,631
1940	4,161	2,897
1950	4,987	3,172
1960	5,559	5,456
1970	7,302	9,367
1980	8,206	12,927
1990	6,433	16,313

7. DECOLONIZATION

Exercise Question: Describe and analyze the various attitudes toward decolonization from 1930 to 1960.

Document A

SOURCE: **Mohandas K. Gandhi, interview with the *Times of India*, March 12, 1930**

In spite of a forest of books containing rules and regulations, the only law the nation knows is the will of the British administrators, and the only public peace the nation knows is the peace of the public prison. India is one vast prison house. I repudiate this law, and regard it as my sacred duty to break the mournful monotony of compulsory peace that is choking the nation's heart for want of a free vent.

Document B

SOURCE: **"Burma: Statement of Policy by His Majesty's Government," May 1945**

The considered policy of His Majesty's Government of promoting full self-government in Burma has frequently been declared. It is and has consistently been our aim to assist her political development till she can sustain the responsibilities of complete self-government within the British Commonwealth.... .

Inevitably Burma's progress towards full self-government has been interrupted and set back by, the Japanese invasion and the long interval of enemy occupation and active warfare in her territories, during which she has suffered grave damage not only in the form of material destruction but in a shattering of the foundations of her economic and social life. It is, of course, upon these foundations that a political structure rests, and until the foundations are once again firm the political institutions which were in operation before the Japanese invasion cannot be restored.... .

Document C

> SOURCE: **President Sukarno of Indonesia, Speech at the opening of the Bandung Conference, April 18, 1955**
>
> All of us, I am certain, are united by more important things than those which superficially divide us. We are united, for instance, by a common detestation of colonialism in whatever form it appears. We are united by a common detestation of racialism. And we are united by a common determination to preserve and stabilise peace in the world. ...
>
> We are often told "Colonialism is dead." Let us not be deceived or even soothed by that. I say to you, colonialism is not yet dead. How can we say it is dead, so long as vast areas of Asia and Africa are unfree.

Document D

> SOURCE: **Prime Minister Nehru, speech to Bandung Conference Political Committee, 1955**
>
> If I join any of these big groups I lose my identity. ... If all the world were to be divided up between these two big blocs what would be the result? The inevitable result would be war. Therefore every step that takes place in reducing that area in the world which may be called the unaligned area is a dangerous step and leads to war... .
>
> Therefore, are we, the countries of Asia and Africa, devoid of any positive position except being pro-communist or anti-communist? Has it come to this, that the leaders of thought who have given religions and all kinds of things to the world have to tag on to this kind of group or that and be hangers-on of this party or the other carrying out their wishes and occasionally giving an idea? It is most degrading and humiliating to any self-respecting people or nation. It is an intolerable thought to me that the great countries of Asia and Africa should come out of bondage into freedom only to degrade themselves or humiliate themselves in this way...

Document E

SOURCE: The "Loi-Cadre," French legislative attempt to resolve the Algerian War, Article 4, June 23, 1956

The Government may ... take all measures intended to raise the standard of living in the territories under the jurisdiction of the Ministry of France Overseas, to promote economic development and social progress and to facilitate economic and financial cooperation between Metropolitan France and those territories, especially:

By generalizing and standardizing education;

By organizing and supporting the production of goods necessary to the economic equilibrium of the territories and to the needs of the franc area; ...

By taking all measures calculated to ensure a successful social program...

Document F

SOURCE: Anwar el Sadat, address delivered at the First Afro-Asian People's Solidarity Conference, December 26, 1957

Because our Conference is a Conference of peoples, it has been able to muster, not only the countries recognized by International Law as independent units, but also those peoples whose status is a foregone conclusion, a historical fact, and a reality endorsed by the whole of mankind, in addition to peoples who are still trodden under the heel of imperialism in one form or another. But our Conference takes the interest of these very peoples to heart. They are the diseased organs in the body of Asia and Africa: consequently they stand in dire need of the greatest of care and attention. A body cannot continue to exist with half of its structure safe and sound while the other half is diseased and decayed... .

Document G

> SOURCE: **United Nations, Declaration on Granting Independence to Colonial Countries and Peoples, 1960**
>
> Recognizing that the peoples of the world ardently desire the end of colonialism in all its manifestations...
>
> Believing that the process of liberation is irresistible and irreversible and that, in order to avoid serious crises, an end must be put to colonialism and all practices of segregation and discrimination associated therewith...
>
> Convinced that all peoples have an inalienable right to complete freedom, the exercise of their sovereignty and the integrity of their national territory,
>
> Solemnly proclaims the necessity of bringing to a speedy and unconditional end colonialism in all its forms and manifestations;
>
> And to this end Declares that ... Inadequacy of political, economic, social or educational preparedness should never serve as a pretext for delaying independence... .

Part A—
Thesis Recognition

Directions: In order to write an excellent thesis, it helps to know what one looks like. The exercise below contains a sample essay question followed by several possible thesis responses. Your job is to score each thesis statement according to the criteria outlined in the new LEQ rubric. Before you begin, review the LEQ rubric guide on page 7 of the Instructional Handbook to familiarize yourself with the thesis qualities that correspond with each score.

Begin each exercise in this set by identifying the tasks and terms of the question (**Step 1**). Next, read the thesis statements below the question. Then, on the line beside each thesis, provide the score that you think it deserves. The new rubric only awards one point for an acceptable thesis, *however*, a strong analytical thesis will help to set the stage for the second Argumentation point, which you will earn in the body of your essay. With that in mind, rate each thesis with a **0**, **1**, or **1+** (for a strong analytical thesis).

1. COLLAPSE OF CLASSICAL EMPIRES

Exercise Question: Analyze the reasons for the decline and collapse of the classical empires in the period from 100 CE to 600 CE.

Possible Thesis Statement Responses:

_____ **A.** Classical Empires like the Han, Gupta, and Roman collapsed by 600 CE because of the constant threat of foreign invaders, the emergence of religious beliefs counter to traditional culture, and the mismanagement of the political administration of the empire.

_____ **B.** Classical Empires like the Han, Gupta, and Roman fell because of their poor economy, government, and military.

_____ **C.** Empires fell for many reasons.

_____ **D.** The Han, Roman, and Gupta empires fell by the end of the classical period.

_____ **E.** The empires in the period from 100 CE to 600 CE collapsed for a variety of reasons.

_____ **F.** The classical empires did not actually fall as evidenced by the persistence of the dynastic system in China, the continuation of Roman tradition in the Byzantine Empire, and the revival of Mayan practices in the Aztec Empire.

_____ **G.** The Han Empire fell because of the corruption of hereditary aristocracy, the rise of non-Chinese leadership and internal rebellion by warlords.

2. CONSEQUENCES OF EXPANDING TRADE

Exercise Question: *Evaluate the effects of expanding trade routes from 600 CE to 1450 CE.*

Possible Thesis Statement Responses:

_____ **A.** There were social, political, and religious effects to the expansion of trade in Africa, Asia, and the Americas.

_____ **B.** The expansion of trade networks in Africa, Asia, and the Americas from 600 CE to 1450 CE created numerous effects related to diffusion of languages like Arabic, the exchange of religious practices like Buddhism, and sharing of technologies like iron works.

_____ **C.** Trade routes had many effects from 600 CE to 1450 CE.

_____ **D.** The various trade routes from 600 CE to 1450 CE had varying effects.

_____ **E.** The Silk Road, Indian Ocean Trade Route, and the Inca Trail had many economic consequences from 600 CE to 1450 CE.

_____ **F.** The expansion of the Indian Ocean Trade Route caused the exchange of iron technology, the diffusion of Islam, and a renaissance in literature.

_____ **G.** New technological improvements, the growth of empire, and the rise of city states caused trade routes to expand in Europe, America, and Africa from 600 to 1450 CE.

3. SHIFT IN EURASIAN INFLUENCES

Exercise Question: Analyze the extent to which the source of influence in Eurasia shifted between 1450 and 1600.

Possible Thesis Statement Responses:

_____ **A.** Power and influence shifted from west to east in Eurasia between 1450 and 1600.

_____ **B.** Although the Italian Renaissance impacted Western art and ideas during this time period, many of the sources of Renaissance thought originated from documents brought west from Constantinople and from ideas shared through interactions with the Chinese and their intermediaries.

_____ **C.** The Renaissance demonstrates that the sources of influence stayed in the West between 1450 and 1600.

_____ **D.** Despite the influx of new ideas from the East as a result of the diaspora caused by the fall of Constantinople, leaders of the Italian Renaissance translated those ideas for the wider European audience and used these eastern concepts to create a movement that was more influential than anything in the original.

_____ **E.** The source of influence in Eurasia shifted to a great extent between 1450 and 1600.

_____ **F.** European powers increased their influence on Eurasia between 1450 and 1600.

_____ **G.** The Ming decision to cease their overseas trade in the mid-1400s led to a sharp decline in Chinese influence on the affairs of other Eurasian kingdoms.

4. INDUSTRIALIZATION AND SOCIAL CHANGE

Exercise Question: *Analyze the impact of the Industrial Revolution on the lower classes of Europe in the 19ᵗʰ century.*

Possible Thesis Statement Responses:

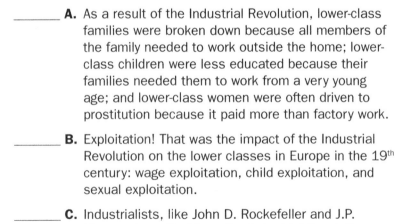

_____ **A.** As a result of the Industrial Revolution, lower-class families were broken down because all members of the family needed to work outside the home; lower-class children were less educated because their families needed them to work from a very young age; and lower-class women were often driven to prostitution because it paid more than factory work.

_____ **B.** Exploitation! That was the impact of the Industrial Revolution on the lower classes in Europe in the 19ᵗʰ century: wage exploitation, child exploitation, and sexual exploitation.

_____ **C.** Industrialists, like John D. Rockefeller and J.P. Morgan, benefited from the Industrial Revolution,

while lower-class people suffered the underside of
the "gilded age."

_____ **D.** The Industrial Revolution affected the living conditions,
working conditions, and social structure of the lower
classes in Europe in the 19th century.

_____ **E.** The Industrial Revolution created several social,
economic, and political disadvantages for lower-class
people in Europe in the 19th century.

_____ **F.** The negative side of the Industrial Revolution hit the
lowest classes the hardest in nineteenth-century
Europe.

_____ **G.** While the Industrial Revolution created new
opportunities for urban workers, low wages and
poor working conditions disadvantaged the lowest
economic classes of nineteenth-century Europe.

5. ITALIAN IMMIGRATION TO ARGENTINA

Exercise Question: *Analyze the extent to which Italian
immigration to Argentina in the late 19th and early 20th centuries
was beneficial to both countries.*

Possible Thesis Statement Responses:

_____ **A.** Italian immigration to Argentina in the 19th and
20th centuries was beneficial to both countries to
a great extent.

_____ **B.** Although Argentina benefited greatly from Italian
immigration in the 19th and 20th centuries, Italy
did not.

_____ **C.** Both countries benefited socially, politically,
and economically.

_____ **D.** Italian immigrants to Argentina brought needed labor
and expertise to help Argentina, while sending their
earnings home to help Italy economically.

_____ **E.** While Argentina may have reaped the greatest benefits from Italian immigration in the 19th and 20th centuries in the form of much-needed agricultural and industrial labor as well as professional expertise, it is also true that Italy's troubled economy benefited from the earnings sent home to support the immigrants' families.

_____ **F.** Italian immigration to Argentina in the designated period may have helped Argentina to build its newly independent economy, but, despite some early benefits associated with the foreign income of these "birds of passage," Italy gained little from the process and lost valuable laborers and professionals.

_____ **G.** Although the Argentine Republic created financial and social incentives to encourage immigration from Europe, it was the weak economy and political disorganization of newly unified Italy that was most responsible for the massive flight of Italians to Argentina in the late 19th and early 20th centuries.

_____ **H.** Argentina benefitted from more people and Italy benefitted from money that was sent home.

6. MUSLIM LEAGUE VS. QUEBECOIS SEPARATISTS

Exercise Question: *In what ways do the Muslim League Movement of British India in the early 1900s and the Quebecois Separatist Movement of Canada from the 1960s share similar motivations?*

Possible Thesis Statement Responses:

_____ **A.** The Muslim League in India and the Quebecois Separatists in Canada were both minority movements based on a perceived lack of adequate political representation, a fear of losing their cultural identities, and a perceived increased in discrimination at the time the movement began.

_____ **B.** The Muslim League and Quebecois Separatists were both interested in seceding from their respective countries, creating new independent constitutions, and conducting their own foreign affairs.

_____ **C.** Both were afraid of losing their independent identities—cultural, social, and political.

_____ **D.** While both wanted to secede from the larger state, the Quebecois Separatists were primarily interested in preserving their language and legal system, and the Muslim League was mostly concerned with religious freedom.

_____ **E.** The Muslim League in India was almost exactly the same as the Quebecois Separatists except for the time period.

_____ **F.** The Muslim League was completely different from the Quebecois Separatists because one wanted independence and the other just wanted more representation.

_____ **G.** They were both politically the same, but economically and socially different.

Part B—
Analytical Thesis Development

Directions: For each of the exercises in this set, follow the model you learned to develop a thesis that answers the question. Be sure to complete each step of the prewriting process to insure that your response is well organized.

Step 1: Identify the tasks and terms
Step 2: Brainstorm specific evidence

Finally, craft your analytical thesis statement.

1. THE NEOLITHIC REVOLUTION

Exercise Question: Analyze the extent to which the Neolithic Revolution served as a cause for the establishment of civilizations.

2. HORTICULTURE TO AGRICULTURE

Exercise Question: Analyze the extent to which agriculture and pastoralism caused transformations in human societies.

3. UNIVERSAL RELIGIONS IN THE CLASSICAL PERIOD

Exercise Question: Analyze the reasons for the rapid expansion of universal religions across Eurasia in the classical period (600 BCE–600 CE).

4. GROWTH OF TRADING CITIES

Exercise Question: *Compare and contrast the reasons for the growth of trading cities in different parts of the world from 600 CE to 1450 CE.*

5. ISLAMIC KINGDOMS

Exercise Question: *Compare and contrast the key characteristics of the two primary Islamic kingdoms of the 16th century, the Ottomans and the Safavids.*

6. INDUSTRIALIZATION OF JAPAN AND BRITAIN

Exercise Question: *Compare and contrast the process of industrialization in Japan with the earlier industrialization of Britain.*

7. INTERWAR ART

Exercise Question: *To what extent was Interwar Art unique from art of the period immediately before World War I?*

8. WWII CONFERENCES AND COLD WAR POLICY

Exercise Question: *Analyze the impact of WWII Allied conferences on subsequent Cold War policy.*

Step

4

Presenting the Argument

Directions: For this set of exercises, you will practice all the skills covered so far in this book:

Step 1: Identify the tasks and terms

Step 2: Brainstorm specific evidence

Step 3: Develop a thesis and categories of evidence, and then outline your argument

Next, use the argument laid out in the given thesis to develop an opening paragraph. Remember that your opening should explain the WHYs and/or HOWs of your categories of evidence and include two or three sentences of historical context. Use the sentences of this paragraph to clearly connect each category of evidence to your main point.

1. COLLAPSE OF CLASSICAL EMPIRES

Exercise Question: *Analyze the reasons for the decline and collapse of the classical empires in the period from 100 CE to 600 CE.*

Thesis: Classical Empires like the Han, Gupta, and Roman collapsed by 600 CE because of the constant threat of foreign invaders, the emergence of religious beliefs counter to traditional culture, and the mismanagement of the political administration of the empire.

2. CONSEQUENCES OF EXPANDING TRADE

Exercise Question: *Evaluate the effects of expanding trade routes from 600 CE to 1450 CE.*

Thesis: The expansion of trade networks in Africa, Asia, and the Americas from 600 CE to 1450 CE created numerous effects related to diffusion of languages like Arabic, the exchange of religious practices like Buddhism, and sharing of technologies like iron works.

3. SHIFT IN EURASIAN INFLUENCES

Exercise Question: *Analyze the extent to which the source of influence in Eurasia shifted between 1450 and 1600.*

Thesis: Despite the influx of new ideas from the East as a result of the diaspora caused by the fall of Constantinople, leaders of the Italian Renaissance translated those ideas for the wider European audience and used these eastern concepts to create a movement that was more influential than anything in the original.

4. INDUSTRIALIZATION AND SOCIAL CHANGE

Exercise Question: *Analyze the impact of the Industrial Revolution on the lower classes of Europe in the 19th century.*

Thesis: As a result of the Industrial Revolution, lower-class families were broken down because all members of the family needed to work outside the home; lower-class children were less educated because their families needed them to work from a very young age; and lower-class women were often driven to prostitution because it paid more than factory work.

5. ITALIAN IMMIGRATION TO ARGENTINA

Exercise Question: Analyze the extent to which Italian immigration to Argentina in the late 19th and early 20th centuries was beneficial to both countries.

Thesis: While Argentina may have reaped the greatest benefits from Italian immigration in the 19th and 20th centuries in the form of much-needed agricultural and industrial labor as well as professional expertise, it is also true that Italy's troubled economy benefited from the earnings sent home to support the immigrants' families.

6. MUSLIM LEAGUE VS. QUEBECOIS SEPARATISTS

Exercise Question: In what ways do the Muslim League Movement of British India in the early 1900s and the Quebecois Separatist Movement of Canada from the 1960s share similar motivations?

Thesis: The Muslim League in India and the Quebecois Separatists in Canada were both minority movements based on a perceived lack of adequate political representation, a fear of losing their cultural identities, and a perceived increase in discrimination at the time the movement began.

Part A—Analyzing Evidence
for the Long Essay Question (LEQ)

Directions: For this set of exercises, you will practice all the skills covered so far in this book:

Step 1: Identify the tasks and terms

Step 2: Brainstorm specific evidence

Step 3: Develop a thesis and categories of evidence, and then outline your argument

Step 4: Write an opening paragraph

Then, using your outline as a guide, write three body paragraphs, remembering that each time you introduce new evidence, you must also explicitly state why it matters to your thesis. Don't worry about writing style, transitions, or the closing—those things will be covered later in the book. Additionally, don't worry about timing and pacing. For now, it is more important to focus all of your attention on developing a written response that meets all the requirements of the AP LEQ rubric.

1. THE EARLIEST URBAN SOCIETIES

Exercise Question: *Evaluate the extent to which the earliest urban societies, 5,000 years ago, laid the foundations for the development of complex civilizations.*

2. THE TRADE NETWORKS OF AFRO-EURASIA

Exercise Question: *Analyze the changes and continuities produced by trade networks throughout Afro-Eurasia from 800 BCE to 900 CE.*

3. CODIFICATION OF RELIGIOUS TRADITIONS

Exercise Question: *To what extent did the codification of religious traditions prior to the first millennium CE mark a turning point in world history?*

4. CONTINUITY AND CHANGE IN DYNASTIC CHINA

Exercise Question: *Describe and explain significant continuities and changes in the Chinese political system from the Tang Dynasty to the Mongol empire.*

5. IMPACT OF TECHNOLOGY, 1900–1918

Exercise Question: *Identify and assess the impact of new technology on the conduct of the Great War.*

6. RAPID ADVANCES IN SCIENCE IN THE 20TH CENTURY

Exercise Question: *Evaluate the extent to which rapid advances in science in the 20th century altered our understanding of the universe and the natural world, and led to the development of new technologies.*

Part B—Analyzing Evidence for the DBQ

Directions: For this set of exercises, you will practice all the skills covered so far in this book:

Step 1: Identify the tasks and terms

Step 2: Brainstorm specific evidence

Step 3: Develop a thesis and categories of evidence, and then outline your argument

Step 4: Write an opening paragraph

Then, using your outline as a guide, write three body paragraphs, remembering that each time you introduce a new document or piece of specific evidence, you must state explicitly why it matters to your thesis. Critically analyze the source wherever you can and, for each document, develop the habit of combining a contextual citation with a sentence-ending parenthetical citation.

1. DAOISM AND CONFUCIANISM

Exercise Question: Compare and contrast the cultural and political effects of Daoism and Confucianism on China.

Document A

SOURCE: **Confucius, *The Analects*, a Confucian text, 500 BCE**

Tzu-kung asked about government. The Master said, "The requisites of government are that there be sufficiency of food, sufficiency of military equipment, and the confidence of the people in their ruler." Tzu Kung said, "If it cannot be helped, and one of these must be dispensed with, which of the three should be foregone first?" "The military equipment," said the Master. Tzu Kung again asked, "If it cannot be helped and one of the remaining two must be dispensed with, which of them should be foregone?" The Master answered, "Part with the food. From of old, death has been the lot of humanity; but if the people have no faith in their rulers, there is no standing for the state."

Chi K'ang-tzu asked Confucius about government, saying, "What do you say to killing unprincipled people for the sake of principled people?" Confucius replied, "Sir, in carrying on your government, why should you use killing at all? Let your evinced desires be for what is good, and the people will be good. The relation between superiors and inferiors is like that between the wind and the grass. The grass must bend, when the wind blows across it."

The Master said, "When a prince's personal conduct is correct, his government is effective without the issuing of orders. If his personal conduct is not correct, he may issue orders, but they will not be followed."

Document B

SOURCE: **Zhuangzi, Daoist philosopher, "The Secret of Caring for Life," c. 360–280 BCE**

Your life has a limit but knowledge has none. If you use what is limited to pursue what has no limit, you will be in danger. If you understand this and still strive for knowledge, you will be in danger for certain! If you do good, stay away from fame. If you do evil, stay away from punishments. Follow the middle; go by what is constant, and you can stay in one piece, keep yourself alive, look after your parents, and live out your years.

Document C

SOURCE: **Xunzi, a Confucian scholar, "Human Nature is Evil,"
c. 250 BCE**

Human nature is evil; its good derives from conscious activity. Now it is human nature to be born with a fondness for profit. Indulging this leads to contention and strife, and the sense of modesty and yielding with which one was born disappears. One is born with feelings of envy and hate, and, by indulging these, one is led into banditry and theft, so that the sense of loyalty and good faith with which he was born disappears. One is born with the desires of the ears and eyes and with a fondness for beautiful sights and sounds, and, by indulging these, one is led to licentiousness and chaos, so that the sense of ritual, rightness, refinement, and principle with which one was born is lost. Hence, following human nature and indulging human emotions will inevitably lead to contention and strife, causing one to rebel against one's proper duty, reduce principle to chaos, and revert to violence. Therefore one must be transformed by the example of a teacher and guided by the way of ritual and rightness before one will attain modesty and yielding, accord with refinement and ritual, and return to order. From this perspective it is apparent that human nature is evil and that its goodness is the result of conscious activity.

A questioner asks: If human nature is evil, then where do ritual and rightness come from? I reply: ritual and rightness are always created by the conscious activity of the sages; essentially they are not created by human nature.

Document D

SOURCE: **Taoist manuscript, ink on silk, unearthed from Han tomb in China, 2nd century BCE**

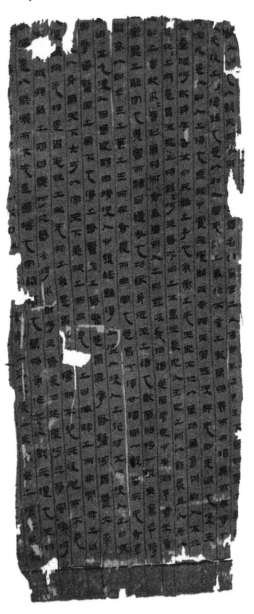

Document E

SOURCE: **Laozi, Tao Te Ching, verse 63, c. 4th century BCE**

Do nondoing,

Strive for nonstriving,

Savour the flavourless,

Regard the small as important,

Make much of little,

Repay enmity with virtue;

Plan for difficulty when it is still easy,

Do the great while it is still small.

The most difficult things in the world

Must be done while they are easy;

The greatest things is the world

Must be done while they are small.

Because of this sages never do great things;

That is why they can fulfill their greatness.

If, in life, you agree too easily you'll be little trusted;

If you take it easy a lot, you'll have a lot of problems.

Therefore it is by managing difficulty

That sages end up without problems.

Document F

SOURCE: **Inscription of the "Five Classics," the Confucian Canon, installed along the road next to the Imperial University, c. 160 CE**

Document G

SOURCE: Yoshotoshi, a Japanese artist, "Zilu, a disciple of Confucius, reading under the moonlight," c. 19th century CE

2. MARGINALIZED PEOPLES

Exercise Question: *Analyze the influence of patriarchy and hierarchy on the treatment of marginalized people from 600 CE to 1450 CE.*

Document A

SOURCE: **Public Letter about Queen Eleanor of Aquitaine following her successful rebellion, written by Peter of Blois at the request of his patron, the Archbishop of Rouen, France, 1173**

Greetings in the search for peace –

Marriage is a firm and indissoluble union. This is public knowledge and no Christian can take the liberty to ignore it. From the beginning biblical truth has verified that marriage once entered into cannot be separated. Truth cannot deceive: it says, "What God has joined let us not put asunder [Matt 19]." Truly, whoever separates a married couple becomes a transgressor of the divine commandment. So the woman is at fault who leaves her husband and fails to keep the trust of this social bond...

We deplore publicly and regretfully that, while you are a most prudent woman [Eleanor of Aquitaine], you have left your husband. The body tears at itself...We know that unless you return to your husband, you will be the cause of widespread disaster. While you alone are now the delinquent one, your actions will result in ruin for everyone in the kingdom. Therefore, illustrious queen, return to your husband and our king. In your reconciliation, peace will be restored from distress, and in your return, joy may return to all...

Truly, you are our parishioner as much as your husband. We cannot fall short in justice: Either you will return to your husband, or we must call upon canon law and use ecclesiastical censures against you. We say this reluctantly, but unless you come back to your senses, with sorrow and tears, we will do so.

Document B

SOURCE: **Ibn Fadlan, an Arab chronicler from Baghdad, from his "Account of the Rus" (Slavic people of modern-day Russia, Ukraine, and Belarus), 921 CE**

I have seen the Rus as they came on their merchant journeys and encamped by the Volga....Each woman wears on either breast a box of iron, silver, copper or gold; the value of the box indicates the wealth of the husband. Each box has a ring from which depends a knife. The women wear neck rings of gold and silver, one for each 10,000 dirhems which her husband is worth; some women have many.

Document C

SOURCE: **The Pact of Umar, Muslim law on the acceptable behavior of Dhimma (Non-Muslims including Jews), c. 7th century CE**

We shall not build, in our cities or in their neighborhood, new monasteries, Churches, convents, or monks' cells, nor shall we repair, by day or by night, such of them as fall in ruins or are situated in the quarters of the Muslims.

We shall keep our gates wide open for passersby and travelers. We shall give board and lodging to all Muslims who pass our way for three days.

We shall not give shelter in our churches or in our dwellings to any spy, nor hide him from the Muslims.

We shall not teach the Qur'an to our children.

We shall not manifest our religion publicly nor convert anyone to it. We shall not prevent any of our kin from entering Islam if they wish it.

We shall show respect toward the Muslims, and we shall rise from our seats when they wish to sit.

We shall not engrave Arabic inscriptions on our seals.

We shall not sell fermented drinks.

We shall not take slaves who have been allotted to Muslims.

Document D

> SOURCE: **Charlemagne, King of the Franks in Europe, Royal Ordinance for the Jews, 814**
>
> 1. Let no Jew presume to take in pledge or for any debt any of the goods of the Church in gold, silver, or other form, from any Christian. But if he presume to do so, which God forbid, let all his goods be seized and let his right hand be cut off.
>
> 2. Let no Jew presume to take any Christian in pledge for any Jew or Christian, nor let him do anything worse; but if he presume to do so, let him make reparation according to his law, and at the same time he shall lose both pledge and debt.
>
> 3. Let no Jew presume to have a money-changer's table in his house, nor shall he presume to sell wine, grain, or other commodities there. But if it be discovered that he has done so all his goods shall be taken away from him, and he shall be imprisoned until he is brought into our presence.

Document E

SOURCE: **Mongolian Class System**

Mongolian Peoples	Hold political positions; given lighter sentences for crimes
Semu Peoples	Hold political positions; given light sentences for crimes
Han Peoples (Northern China)	Forbidden to own a weapon; given strict sentences for crimes
Southern Peoples (Formerly Song Dynasty)	Forbidden to own a weapon; given strictest sentences for crimes

Document F

SOURCE: **February in the *Book of Hours*, Painted by the Limbourg Brothers for their patron the Duke of Berry, c. 1412**

Document G

SOURCE: **Illustration of the Incan Mit'a System, Laborers using Seed Drill, date unknown**

3. THE CONCEPT OF LOVE

Exercise Question: *Compare and contrast the concept of "love" across Eurasia and the ways in which it impacted gender relations from 400 to 1300 CE.*

Document A

SOURCE: **Kalidasa, Indian dramatist, from *Shakuntala*, c. 400 CE**

SHAKUNTALA (*miming what Primayada described*): Listen and tell me if this makes sense!

BOTH FRIENDS: We're both paying attention.

SHAKUNTALA (*sings*): I don't know your heart, but day and night Love violently burns my limbs with desire for you, cruel man.

KING (*having been listening to them, entering suddenly*): Love torments you, slender girl, but he utterly consumes me—daylight makes the moon fade when it folds the white lotus.

BOTH FRIENDS (*looking, rising with delight*): Welcome to the swift success of love's desire! (*Shakuntala tries to rise*)

KING: Don't strain yourself! Limbs on a couch of crushed flowers and fragrant tips of lotus stalks are too frail from suffering to perform ceremonial acts…

ANASUYA: We've heard that kings have many loves. Will our beloved friend become a sorrow to her relatives after you've spent your time with her?

KING: Noble lady, enough of this! I may have many wives, but my royal line rests on two foundations: the sea-bound earth and this friend of yours!

BOTH FRIENDS: We are assured…

SHAKUNTALA: Come back! Don't leave me unprotected!

Document B

> SOURCE: **Procopius, Byzantine historian, writing about the life of Empress Theodora, from *The Secret History*, c. 550-560**
>
> [Justinian] took a wife: and in what manner she was born and bred, and, wedded to this man, tore up the Roman Empire by the very roots, I shall now relate.
>
> Acacius was the keeper of wild beasts used in the amphitheater in Constantinople; he belonged to the Green faction and was nicknamed the Bearkeeper. This man, during the rule of Anastasius, fell sick and died, leaving three daughters named Comito, Theodora, and Anastasia: of whom the eldest was not yet seven years old.... When these children reached the age of girlhood, their mother put them on the local stage.... Comito, indeed, had already become one of the leading hetaerae (prostitutes) of the day.
>
> Theodora, the second sister, dressed in a little tunic with sleeves, like a slave girl, waited on Comito and used to follow her about carrying on her shoulders the bench on which her favored sister was wont to sit at public gatherings. Now Theodora was still too young to know the normal relation of man with maid, but consented to the unnatural violence of villainous slaves who, following their masters to the theater, employed their leisure in this infamous manner. And for some time in a brothel she suffered such misuse.
>
> But as soon as she arrived at the age of youth, and was now ready for the world, her mother put her on the stage. Forthwith, she became a courtesan, and such as the ancient Greeks used to call a common one, at that: for she was not a flute or harp player, nor was she even trained to dance, but only gave her youth to anyone she met, in utter abandonment.... On the field of pleasure she was never defeated. Often she would go picnicking with ten young men or more, in the flower of the strength and virility, and dallied with them all, the whole night through. When they wearied of the sport, she would approach their servants....
>
> But when she came back to Constantinople, Justinian fell violently in love with her. At first he kept her only as a mistress, though he raised her to patrician rank. Through him Theodora was able immediately to acquire an unholy power and exceedingly great riches....

Document C

SOURCE: from *1001 Arabian Nights*, a collection of stories of unknown origin and authorship, probably first assembled in Persia about the 9th century CE

In the chronicles of the ancient dynasty of the Sassanian, who reigned for about four hundred years, from Persia to the borders of China, beyond the great river Ganges itself, we read the praises of one of the kings of this race, who was said to be the best monarch of his time. His subjects loved him, and his neighbors feared him, and when he died he left his kingdom in a more prosperous and powerful condition than any king had done before him.

The two sons who survived him loved each other tenderly, and it was a real grief to the elder, Schahriar, that the laws of the empire forbade him to share his dominions with his brother Schahzeman. Indeed, after ten years, during which this state of things had not ceased to trouble him, Schahriar cut off the country of Great Tartary from the Persian Empire and made his brother king.

Now the Sultan Schahriar had a wife whom he loved more than all the world, and his greatest happiness was to surround her with splendor, and to give her the finest dresses and the most beautiful jewels. It was therefore with the deepest shame and sorrow that he accidentally discovered, after several years, that she had deceived him completely, and her whole conduct turned out to have been so bad, that he felt himself obliged to carry out the law of the land, and order the grand-vizier to put her to death. The blow was so heavy that his mind almost gave way, and he declared that he was quite sure that at bottom all women were as wicked as the sultana, if you could only find them out, and that the fewer the world contained the better. So every evening he married a fresh wife and had her strangled the following morning before the grand-vizier, whose duty it was to provide these unhappy brides for the Sultan. The poor man fulfilled his task with reluctance, but there was no escape, and every day saw a girl married and a wife dead.

Document D

SOURCE: **Murasaki Shikibu, a woman at the Japanese court, from** *The Tale of Genji,* **c. 1000 CE**

The festival ended late that night. Once the senior nobles had withdrawn, once the Empress and the Heir Apparent were gone and all lay quiet in the beauty of brilliant moonlight, Genji remained drunkenly unwilling to grant that the night was over. His Majesty's gentlewomen all being asleep, he stole off ... to the long aisle of the Kokiden, where he found the third door open. Hardly anyone seemed to be about, since the Consort had gone straight to wait on His Majesty. The door to the inner rooms was open, too. There was no sound.

This is how people get themselves into trouble, he thought, stepping silently up into the hall. Everyone must be asleep.... He happily caught her sleeve.

"Oh, don't! Who are you?" She was obviously frightened.

"You need not be afraid." With this he put his arms around her, lay her down, and closed the door. Her outrage and dismay gave her delicious appeal.

"A man—there is a man here!" she cried, trembling.

"I may do as a I please, and calling for help will not save you. Just be still!"

She knew his voice and felt a little better. She did not want to seem cold or standoffish, despite her shock. He must have been quite drunk, because he felt he must have her, and she was young and pliant enough that she probably never thought seriously of resisting him.

Document E

SOURCE: Andreas Capellanus, aka Andreas the Chaplain, French author, from *The Art of Courtly Love*, 1184-86

Love is a certain inborn suffering derived from the sight of and excessive meditation upon the beauty of the opposite sex, which causes each one to wish above all things the embraces of the other and by common desire to carry out all of love's precepts in the other's embrace....

If one of the lovers should be unfaithful to the other, and the offender is the man, and he has an eye to a new love affair, he renders himself wholly unworthy of his former love, and she ought to deprive him completely of her embraces....

But what if he should be unfaithful to his beloved – not with the idea of finding a new love, but because he has been driven to it by an irresistible passion for another woman? What, for instance, if chance should present to him an unknown woman in a convenient place or what if at a time when Venus is urging him on to that which I am talking about he should meet with a little strumpet or somebody's servant girl? Should he, just because he played with her in the grass, lose the love of his beloved? We can say without fear of contradiction that just for this a lover is not considered unworthy of the love of his beloved unless he indulges in so many excesses with a number of women that we may conclude that he is overpassionate....

Document F

> SOURCE: **Ulrich von Liechtenstein, Austrian minor noble, speaking of a woman he admires and then of his wife, from his autobiography,** *The Service of Ladies,* **1255**
>
> If you would please me, messenger,
> then travel once again to her.
> Just tell her what I have in mind
> and ask if she would be so kind
> as to permit that I should fight
> throughout this journey as her knight.
> It's something she will not repent
> and I'll be glad of her assent.
>
> He rode at once to tell her this
> and swore upon his hope of bliss
> my loyalty would never falter,
> that I was true and would not alter.
> He told my plan in full detail
> and said, "My lady, should you fail
> to let him serve and show your trust
> in him, it wouldn't seem quite just."
> …
>
> I changed my clothing under guard,
> and then the hostel door was barred.
> I took with me a servant who
> would not say anything, I knew.
> We stole away without a sound
> and rode with joy to where I found
> my dearest wife whom I adore;
> I could not ever love her more.
>
> She greeted me just as a good
> and loving woman always should
> receive a husband she holds dear.
> That I had come to see her here
> had made her really very pleased.
> My visit stilled her grief and eased
> her loneliness. We shared our bliss,
> my sweet and I, with many a kiss.

Document G

> SOURCE: **Zhou Daguan, traveler to Cambodia on behalf of Emperor Temur Khan (Kubilai Khan's grandson), from** *Sex in the City of Angkor,* **1297**
>
> When a family is bringing up a daughter, her father and mother are sure to wish her well by saying, "May you have what really matters – in future may you marry thousands and thousands of husbands!"
>
> When they are seven to nine years old – if they are girls from wealthy homes – or only when they are eleven – if they come from the poorest families – girls have to get a Buddhist monk or a Daoist to take away their virginity, in what is called *zhentan*.

4. ITALIAN IMMIGRATION TO ARGENTINA

Exercise Question: *Analyze the extent to which Italian immigration to Argentina in the late 19th and early 20th centuries was beneficial to both countries.*

Document A

SOURCE: **from Argentina's National Constitution, 1853 (reinstated in 1983 and amended through 1994)**

We, the representatives of the people of the Argentine Nation, assembled in General Constituent Congress by the will and election of the provinces which compose it, in fulfillment of pre-existing pacts, with the object of constituting the national union, ensuring justice, preserving domestic peace, providing for the common defense, promoting the general welfare, and securing the blessings of liberty to ourselves, to our posterity, and to all men in the world who wish to dwell on Argentine soil: invoking the protection of God, source of all reason and justice, do ordain, decree and establish this Constitution for the Argentine Nation.

Part 1

Chapter I: Declarations, Rights, and Guarantees

...

Article 23

The Federal Government shall encourage European immigration, and it may not restrict, limit, or burden with any tax whatsoever the entry into Argentine territory of foreigners whose purpose is tilling the soil, improving industries, and introducing and teaching the sciences and the arts.

Document B

SOURCE: **J. H. Senner, Commissioner of Immigration at the Port of New York, from "Immigration from Italy,"** *The North American Review*, 1896

The Italians only, of all the Latin peoples, developed a tendency to migration ... and until a very recent date such immigration into the United States was very much smaller than that into the southern part of the Western Continent, especially the Argentine Republic.... Poor Italy had suffered perpetually from misrule and bloody wars and consequent commercial depression. United Italy, only a little more than a quarter of a century in existence, could not as yet succeed in securing safety, peace, and welfare to her subjects ... refrained from opposing such emigration, and has even seemingly favored it.

For a good many years this policy of the Italian Government seemed to produce advantageous results to the prosperity of Italy. As long as the migration to and fro was entirely unrestricted, Italians in large numbers were in the habit of crossing and recrossing the ocean, some as many as ten times, as so-called "birds of passage," and taking out of the United States, or other countries of America, the gains which their standard of living, far below that of an American wage earner, made it easy for them to accumulate. The amount of money annually sent home by Italian laborers or taken back by them has been conservatively estimated at from $4,000,000 to even $30,000,000.... But these advantages to the old country are about to cease definitely. The rigid enforcement of the Federal statutes since 1893 by the United States Immigration Officials has made it very hard for Italian " birds of passage" to come and go at their pleasure. Besides, quite a large proportion of those who originally came to the United States with no intention of acquiring residence, found the country so advantageous and congenial to them that they changed their minds, sent for their families and settled permanently within the United States, acquiring, in time, rights of citizenship.

Document C

SOURCE: **Walter F. Willcox, an American statistician and pioneer of demography, from a collection of immigration statistics in Argentina, Brazil, Paraguay, Uruguay, Chile published in** *International Migrations, Volume I: Statistics,* **1929**

Table III—Distribution, by Occupation, of Immigrant Aliens
(2nd & 3rd Class Passengers), by Sea (in Decades), 1857–1924

Year	Total	Agriculture	Industry and Mining	Transport and Commerce	Domestic Service and General Labor	Liberal Professions and Public Services	Other occupations, none, or unknown
1857-1860	20,000	9,421	1,105	823	1,850	124	6,677
1861-1870	159,570	77,671	4,699	4,053	16,373	554	56,220
1871-1880	260,885	100,701	18,319	8,653	24,780	2,064	106,368
1881-1890	841,122	454,919	67,686	26,217	93,115	5,288	193,897
1891-1900	648,326	288,429	50,613	29,068	127,415	4,364	148,437
1901-1910	1,764,103	562,884	161,092	107,983	493,685	14,248	424,211
1911-1920	1,204,919	211,061	99,858	75,289	449,196	16,789	352,726
1921-1924	582,351	142,838	71,187	48,888	125,120	11,854	181,864

Document D

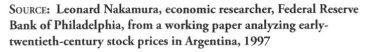

SOURCE: **Leonard Nakamura, economic researcher, Federal Reserve Bank of Philadelphia, from a working paper analyzing early-twentieth-century stock prices in Argentina, 1997**

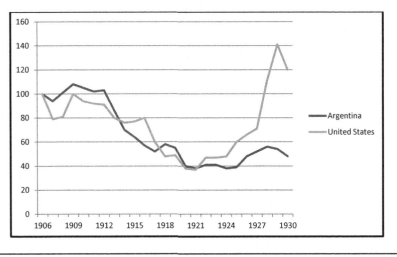

Document E

SOURCE: Daniela Del Boca, Professor of Economics, University of Torino, from a discussion paper analyzing Italian emigration patterns, 2003

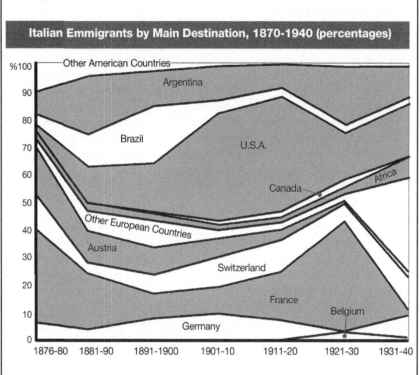

Italian Emmigrants by Main Destination, 1870-1940 (percentages)

Document F

SOURCE: **from "Argentina – Overview of the History of International Migration in Argentina," a report summarizing immigration statistics for the history of Argentina, published by the Organization of American States, 2014**

After obtaining its independence from Spain at the beginning of the 19th century, Argentina adopted an open immigration policy and encouraged immigrants to adopt the country as their own. For a brief period of time at the end of the 1880s, the government subsidized passage tickets for immigrants. It is estimated that the country received more than seven million immigrants between 1870 and 1930, mainly from Spain and Italy. The reasons for this mass exodus from Europe are several.... In the case of the Italian immigrants, Argentina promised to be a new opportunity as they left behind a country impoverished by the unification of the Italian states where unemployment, overpopulation, and serious political conflicts prevailed.

Massive immigrations from Europe responded in part to the offer of better wages. On average, a farm worker earned in four or five months of harvesting, between five and ten times more than what he/she earned in his/her country of origin. Another point of attraction was government programs. In 1862, [Argentina's] Congress authorized the hiring of immigrants to colonize national territories, specifically the regions external to the constituted provinces that were governed from Buenos Aires. The Office of Migration (Dirección de Migraciones), established in 1869, appointed agents in Europe to recruit colonists. The new arrivals enjoyed free accommodations, tax exemption on their possessions, and also, as time evolved, free rail transportation. Many of the first immigrants achieved quick social mobility; although very few were able to acquire lands.

In 1854, Buenos Aires had a population of 90,000 inhabitants; towards 1869, the population increased to 177,000, including 41,000 Italians and 20,000 Spaniards; in 1895, the number rose to 670,000. In 1914, the immigrant population represented 30% of the total population. In Buenos Aires, estimates of the immigrant population ... vary between 60% and 80%....

Document G

SOURCE: Jutta Bolt, Professor of Economics, Lund University, Netherlands, from "GDP per Capita since 1820," in *How Was Life?: Global Well-being since 1820*, 2014

GDP per Capita (USD)

Decade	Argentina	Italy
1820	998	1,511
1830	---	1,507
1840	---	1,537
1850	1,251	1,481
1860	1,355	1,459
1870	1,468	1,542
1880	1,604	1,589
1890	2,416	1,690
1900	2,875	1,855
1910	3,822	2,176
1920	3,473	2,153
1930	4,080	2,631
1940	4,161	2,897
1950	4,987	3,172
1960	5,559	5,456
1970	7,302	9,367
1980	8,206	12,927
1990	6,433	16,313

5. DENG XIAOPING IN CHINA'S ECONOMIC LIBERALIZATION

Exercise Question: Analyze the role of Deng Xiaoping in China's economic liberalization beginning in the late 1970s.

Document A

SOURCE: **Clem Tisdell, Professor Emeritus, School of Economics, The University of Queensland (Australia), from "Economic reform and openness in China: China's development policies in the last 30 years," an article in** *Economic Analysis and Policy,* **2009**

Several other important decisions about reforms were made at the Third Plenary Session. There was recognition of the need to reduce bureaucratic centralized management of the economy and eliminate bureaucratic and political impediments to achieving economic efficiency and development, particularly at lower levels (such as local levels) of economic activity. This was consistent with Deng Xiaoping's emphasis on professionalism and efficient economic management. It was decided that the economic reforms should begin with agriculture because at that time it was "the foundation of the national economy". Particular attention was given to the rule of law, decentralization and resource ownership in undertaking the agricultural reforms. These features were applied later to the rest of the economy. Again, in line with the views of Deng Xiaoping, it was agreed that economic incentives should be incorporated in the economic system and that economic responsibility should be stressed. The principle of "each according to his work" should be followed rather than the principle of "each according to his need". It was stated that in order to promote production, it is necessary "to work out payment in accordance with the amount and quality of work done, and avoid equalitarianism". This represented a major departure from the previous "iron bowl" policy which emphasized egalitarianism.

Document B

SOURCE: Deng Xiaoping, from a speech, "Uphold the Four Basic Principles," delivered 30 March 1979

The [Party] Center believes that in realizing the four modernizations in China we must uphold the four basic principles in thought and politics. They are the fundamental premise for realizing the four modernizations. They are:

1. We must uphold the socialist road.

2. We must uphold the dictatorship of the proletariat.

3. We must uphold the leadership of the Communist Party.

4. We must uphold Marxism-Leninism and Mao Zedong Thought.

The Center believes that we must reemphasize upholding the four basic principles today because some people (albeit an extreme minority) have attempted to shake those basic principles. ... Realizing the four modernizations is a many-sided complex and difficult undertaking. The task of the ideological and theoretical workers cannot be confined to discussion of the basic principles. We are confronted with many questions of economic theory, including both basic theory and theory applied to particular spheres such as industry, agriculture, commerce and management. Lenin called for more talk about economics and less about politics. In my opinion, his words are still applicable with regard to the proportion of effort that should be devoted to theoretical work in these two spheres. I am not saying of course that there are no more questions to be studied in the political field. For many years we have neglected the study of political science, law, sociology and world politics, and now we must hurry to make up our deficiencies in these subjects. Most of our ideological and theoretical workers should dig into one or more specialized subjects. All those who can do so should learn foreign languages, so as to be able to read important foreign works on the social sciences without difficulty. We have admitted that we lag behind many countries in our study of the natural sciences. Now we should admit that we also lag behind in our study of the social sciences, insofar as they are comparable in China and abroad. Our level is very low and for years we haven't even had adequate statistical data in the social sciences, a lack that is naturally a great obstacle to any serious study.

Document C

> SOURCE: **Agreement of Xiaogang Farmers, translation by Alex Tabarrok, Professor of Economics at George Mason University, from "The Secret Agreement that Revolutionized China," 2012**
>
>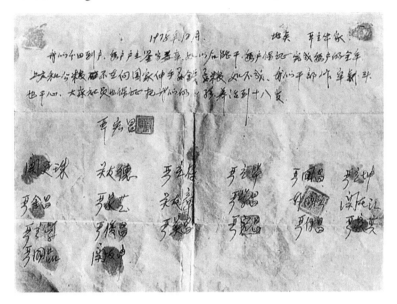
>
> Literal Translation: December 1978 Mr. Yan's Home -- We divide the field (land) to every household. Every leader of the household should sign and stamp. If we are able to produce, every household should promise to finish any amount they are required to turn into the government, no longer asking the government for food or money. If this fails, even if we go to jail or have our heads shaved, we will not regret. Everyone else (the common people who are not officers and signees of this agreement) also promise to raise our children until they are eighteen years old.

Document D

SOURCE: Alex Tabarrok, Professor of Economics at George Mason University, from "The Secret Agreement that Revolutionized China," 2012

The Great Leap Forward was a great leap backward – agricultural land was less productive in 1978 than it had been in 1949 when the communists took over. In 1978, however, farmers in the village of Xiaogang held a secret meeting. The farmers agreed to divide the communal land and assign it to individuals – each farmer had to produce a quota for the government but anything he or she produced in excess of the quota they would keep. The agreement violated government policy and as a result the farmers also pledged that if any of them were to be killed or jailed the others would raise his or her children until the age of 18.

The change from collective property rights to something closer to private property rights had an immediate effect, investment, work effort and productivity increased. "You can't be lazy when you work for your family and yourself," said one of the farmers.

Word of the secret agreement leaked out and local bureaucrats cut off Xiaogang from fertilizer, seeds and pesticides. But amazingly, before Xiaogang could be stopped, farmers in other villages also began to abandon collective property. In Beijing, Mao Zedong was dead and a new set of rulers, seeing the productivity improvements, decided to let the experiment proceed.

Document E

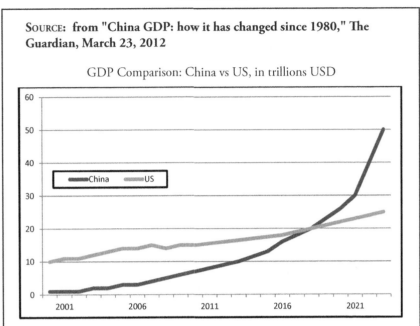

SOURCE: from "China GDP: how it has changed since 1980," The Guardian, March 23, 2012

GDP Comparison: China vs US, in trillions USD

Document F

SOURCE: **Tomas Hirst, Editorial director and co-founder of *Pieria* magazine, from his article for the World Economic Forum, "A Brief History of China's Economic Growth," 2015**

According to the authors, the Third Plenary Session of the 11th Central Committee of the Communist Party in December 1978 was the defining moment in shifting the country from its unsteady early economic trajectory on to a more sustainable path. It laid the groundwork for future growth by introducing reforms that allowed farmers to sell their produce in local markets and began the shift from collective farming to the household responsibility system.

A year later the Law on Chinese Foreign Equity Joint Ventures was introduced, allowing foreign capital to enter China helping to boost regional economies although it took until the mid-1980s for the government to gradually ease pricing restrictions and allow companies to retain profits and set up their own wage structures. This not only helped to boost GDP from an annual average of 6% between 1953–1978 to 9.4% between 1978–2012 but also increased the pace of urbanization as workers were drawn from the countryside into higher-paying jobs in cities.

This process of market liberalization led to the establishment of China as a major global exporter. It eventually allowed for the reopening of the Shanghai stock exchange in December 1990 for the first time in over 40 years and, ultimately, to China's accession to the World Trade Organization

These reforms had a significant impact both on per capita GDP and the pace of the falling share of the labor force working in agriculture.

Document G

> **SOURCE: Report from the Third Plenary Session of the 11th Central Committee of the Communist Party of China, December, 1978**
>
> The plenary session holds that the whole Party should concentrate its main energy and efforts on advancing agriculture as fast as possible because agriculture, the foundation of the national economy, has been seriously damaged in recent years and remains very weak on the whole. The rapid development of the national economy as a whole and the steady improvement in the living standards of the people of the whole country depends on the vigorous restoration and speeding up of farm production.... This requires first of all releasing the socialist enthusiasm of our country's several hundred million peasants, paying full attention to their material well-being economically and giving effective protection to their democratic rights politically. Taking this as the guideline, the plenary session set forth a series of policies and economic measures aimed at raising present agricultural production. The most important are as follows: The right of ownership by the people's communes ... and their power of decision must be protected effectively by the laws of the state; it is not permitted to commandeer the manpower, funds, products and material of any production team; the economic organizations at various levels of the people's commune must conscientiously implement the socialist principle of "to each according to his work," work out payment in accordance with the amount and quality of work done, and overcome equalitarianism; small plots of land for private use by commune members, their domestic side-occupations, and village fairs are necessary adjuncts of the socialist economy, and must not be interfered with....

Part C—Analytical Transitions

Directions: For each of the following exercises, you will continue to practice all the skills covered so far in this book:

Step 1: Identify the tasks and terms

Step 2: Brainstorm specific evidence (and analyze the documents in the DBQ)

Step 3: Develop a thesis and categories of evidence, and then outline your argument

Step 4: Write an opening paragraph

Step 5: Analyze your specific evidence in three body paragraphs

Then, using the example from the Instructional Handbook as a model, write transition sentences to analytically connect the ideas within your body paragraphs. Remember that transitions are not simply exercises in good writing style, but can be effective tools of analysis as well. Your transitions should connect the main ideas of your argument.

1. IMPACT ON ENVIRONMENT OF HUNTER-FORAGERS AND SETTLED SOCIETIES

Exercise Question: Contrast how hunter-foragers and settled societies affected the environment.

2. EXPANSION OF ISLAM

Exercise Question: Assess the extent to which the promotion of Islam changed trade, warfare, and culture from 700 CE to 1453 CE.

3. THE COLUMBIAN EXCHANGE

Exercise Question: *To what extent was the Columbian Exchange mutually beneficial to Native Americans and Europeans?*

Document A

> SOURCE: **Pope Paul III, in a decree, 1537**
>
> … all Indians are truly men, not only capable of understanding the Catholic faith, but … exceedingly desirous to receive it.

Document B

> SOURCE: **Domingo Martínez de Irala, first governor of Paraguay, message left for his successor, 1542**
>
> In one of the islands of San Gabriel a sow and a boar have been left to breed. Do not kill them. If there should be many, take those you need, but always leave some to breed, and also, on your way, leave a sow and a boar on the island of Martin Garcia and on the other islands wherever you think it good, so that they may breed.

Document C

> SOURCE: **Anonymous aborigine of Yucatan, speaking of pre-Spanish life, c. 1550**
>
> There was then no sickness; they had no aching bones; they had then no high fever; they had then no smallpox; they had then no burning chest; they had then no abdominal pain; they had then no consumption; they had then no headache. At that time the course of humanity was orderly. The foreigners made it otherwise when they arrived here.

Document D

SOURCE: **Thomas Hariot, naturalist, on his voyage to Roanoke, 1585**

… within a few days after our departure … people began to die very fast, and many in short space; in some towns about twenty, in some forty, in some sixty, & in one six score, which in truth was very many in respect to their numbers. … The disease was also so strange that they neither knew what it was, nor how to cure it; the like by report of the oldest men in the country never happened before… .

Document E

SOURCE: **John Gerard, English plant expert, *Herball, Generall Historie of Plants,* 1597**

We have as yet no certain proof or experience concerning the virtues of this kind of Corn, although the barbarous Indians which know no better are constrained to make a virtue of necessity, and think it a good food: whereas we may easily judge that it nourishes but little, and is of a hard and evil digestion, a more convenient food for swine than for man.

Document F

SOURCE: **Anonymous German missionary to the New World, 1699**

…the Indians die so easily that the bare look and smell of a Spaniard causes them to give up the ghost.

Document G

SOURCE: **Anonymous German missionary to the New World, 1699**

A Comanche on his feet is out of his element, and comparatively almost as awkward as a monkey on the ground, without a limb or a branch to cling to; but the moment he lays his hand upon his horse, his face even becomes handsome, and he gracefully flies away like a different being.

4. ITALIAN IMMIGRATION TO ARGENTINA

Exercise Question: *Analyze the extent to which Italian immigration to Argentina in the late 19th and early 20th centuries was beneficial to both countries.*

Document A

SOURCE: **from Argentina's National Constitution, 1853 (reinstated in 1983 and amended through 1994)**

We, the representatives of the people of the Argentine Nation, assembled in General Constituent Congress by the will and election of the provinces which compose it, in fulfillment of pre-existing pacts, with the object of constituting the national union, ensuring justice, preserving domestic peace, providing for the common defense, promoting the general welfare, and securing the blessings of liberty to ourselves, to our posterity, and to all men in the world who wish to dwell on Argentine soil: invoking the protection of God, source of all reason and justice, do ordain, decree and establish this Constitution for the Argentine Nation.

Part 1

Chapter I: Declarations, Rights, and Guarantees

...

Article 23

The Federal Government shall encourage European immigration, and it may not restrict, limit, or burden with any tax whatsoever the entry into Argentine territory of foreigners whose purpose is tilling the soil, improving industries, and introducing and teaching the sciences and the arts.

Document B

SOURCE: **J. H. Senner, Commissioner of Immigration at the Port of New York, from "Immigration from Italy,"** *The North American Review,* **1896**

The Italians only, of all the Latin peoples, developed a tendency to migration ... and until a very recent date such immigration into the United States was very much smaller than that into the southern part of the Western Continent, especially the Argentine Republic.... Poor Italy had suffered perpetually from misrule and bloody wars and consequent commercial depression. United Italy, only a little more than a quarter of a century in existence, could not as yet succeed in securing safety, peace, and welfare to her subjects ... refrained from opposing such emigration, and has even seemingly favored it.

For a good many years this policy of the Italian Government seemed to produce advantageous results to the prosperity of Italy. As long as the migration to and fro was entirely unrestricted, Italians in large numbers were in the habit of crossing and recrossing the ocean, some as many as ten times, as so-called "birds of passage," and taking out of the United States, or other countries of America, the gains which their standard of living, far below that of an American wage earner, made it easy for them to accumulate. The amount of money annually sent home by Italian laborers or taken back by them has been conservatively estimated at from $4,000,000 to even $30,000,000.... But these advantages to the old country are about to cease definitely. The rigid enforcement of the Federal statutes since 1893 by the United States Immigration Officials has made it very hard for Italian " birds of passage" to come and go at their pleasure. Besides, quite a large proportion of those who originally came to the United States with no intention of acquiring residence, found the country so advantageous and congenial to them that they changed their minds, sent for their families and settled permanently within the United States, acquiring, in time, rights of citizenship.

Document C

SOURCE: **Walter F. Willcox, an American statistician and pioneer of demography, from a collection of immigration statistics in Argentina, Brazil, Paraguay, Uruguay, Chile published in** *International Migrations, Volume I: Statistics,* **1929**

Table III—Distribution, by Occupation, of Immigrant Aliens
(2nd & 3rd Class Passengers), by Sea (in Decades), 1857–1924

Year	Total	Agriculture	Industry and Mining	Transport and Commerce	Domestic Service and General Labor	Liberal Professions and Public Services	Other occupations, none, or unknown
1857-1860	20,000	9,421	1,105	823	1,850	124	6,677
1861-1870	159,570	77,671	4,699	4,053	16,373	554	56,220
1871-1880	260,885	100,701	18,319	8,653	24,780	2,064	106,368
1881-1890	841,122	454,919	67,686	26,217	93,115	5,288	193,897
1891-1900	648,326	288,429	50,613	29,068	127,415	4,364	148,437
1901-1910	1,764,103	562,884	161,092	107,983	493,685	14,248	424,211
1911-1920	1,204,919	211,061	99,858	75,289	449,196	16,789	352,726
1921-1924	582,351	142,838	71,187	48,888	125,120	11,854	181,864

Document D

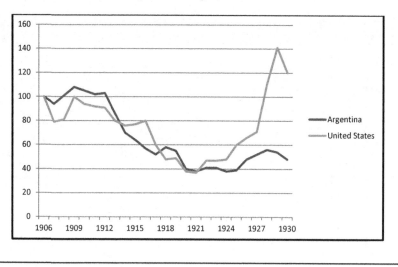

SOURCE: Leonard Nakamura, economic researcher, Federal Reserve Bank of Philadelphia, from a working paper analyzing early-twentieth-century stock prices in Argentina, 1997

Document E

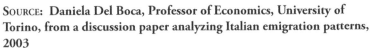

SOURCE: **Daniela Del Boca, Professor of Economics, University of Torino, from a discussion paper analyzing Italian emigration patterns, 2003**

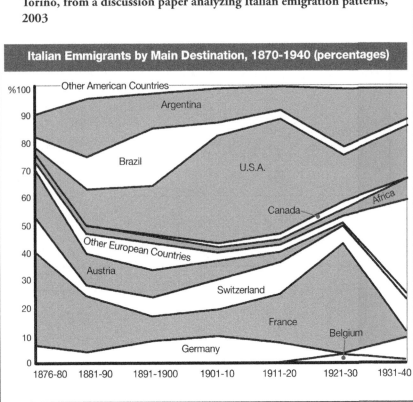

Italian Emmigrants by Main Destination, 1870-1940 (percentages)

Document F

SOURCE: from "Argentina – Overview of the History of International Migration in Argentina," a report summarizing immigration statistics for the history of Argentina, published by the Organization of American States, 2014

After obtaining its independence from Spain at the beginning of the 19th century, Argentina adopted an open immigration policy and encouraged immigrants to adopt the country as their own. For a brief period of time at the end of the 1880s, the government subsidized passage tickets for immigrants. It is estimated that the country received more than seven million immigrants between 1870 and 1930, mainly from Spain and Italy. The reasons for this mass exodus from Europe are several…. In the case of the Italian immigrants, Argentina promised to be a new opportunity as they left behind a country impoverished by the unification of the Italian states where unemployment, overpopulation, and serious political conflicts prevailed.

Massive immigrations from Europe responded in part to the offer of better wages. On average, a farm worker earned in four or five months of harvesting, between five and ten times more than what he/she earned in his/her country of origin. Another point of attraction was government programs. In 1862, [Argentina's] Congress authorized the hiring of immigrants to colonize national territories, specifically the regions external to the constituted provinces that were governed from Buenos Aires. The Office of Migration (Dirección de Migraciones), established in 1869, appointed agents in Europe to recruit colonists. The new arrivals enjoyed free accommodations, tax exemption on their possessions, and also, as time evolved, free rail transportation. Many of the first immigrants achieved quick social mobility; although very few were able to acquire lands.

In 1854, Buenos Aires had a population of 90,000 inhabitants; towards 1869, the population increased to 177,000, including 41,000 Italians and 20,000 Spaniards; in 1895, the number rose to 670,000. In 1914, the immigrant population represented 30% of the total population. In Buenos Aires, estimates of the immigrant population … vary between 60% and 80%….

Document G

SOURCE: Jutta Bolt, Professor of Economics, Lund University, Netherlands, from "GDP per Capita since 1820," in *How Was Life?: Global Well-being since 1820*, 2014

GDP per Capita (USD)

Decade	Argentina	Italy
1820	998	1,511
1830	---	1,507
1840	---	1,537
1850	1,251	1,481
1860	1,355	1,459
1870	1,468	1,542
1880	1,604	1,589
1890	2,416	1,690
1900	2,875	1,855
1910	3,822	2,176
1920	3,473	2,153
1930	4,080	2,631
1940	4,161	2,897
1950	4,987	3,172
1960	5,559	5,456
1970	7,302	9,367
1980	8,206	12,927
1990	6,433	16,313

5. THE BOER WAR

Exercise Question: Analyze the ways in which the Boer War was portrayed in published works.

Document A

Source: **Richard Harding Davis, from *With Both Armies in South Africa*, 1900**

Just as they had reached the centre of the town, General Sir George White and his staff rode down from headquarters and met the men whose coming meant for him life and peace and success. They were advancing at a walk, with the cheering people hanging to their stirrups, clutching at their hands and hanging to the bridles of their horses.

General White's first greeting was characteristically unselfish and loyal, and typical of the British officer. He gave no sign of his own incalculable relief, nor did he give to Caesar the things which were Caesar's. He did not cheer Dundonald, nor Buller, nor the column which had rescued him and his garrison from present starvation and probable imprisonment at Pretoria. He raised his helmet and cried, "We will give three cheers for the Queen!" And then the General and the healthy ragged and sunburned troopers from the outside world, the starved, fever-ridden garrison and the starved, fever-ridden civilians stood with hats off and sang their national anthem.

The column outside had been fighting steadily for six weeks to get Dundonald or any one of its force into Ladysmith; for fourteen days it had been living in the open, fighting by night as well as by day, without halt or respite; the garrison inside had been for four months holding the enemy at bay with the point of the bayonet; it was famished for food, it was rotten with fever, and yet when the relief came and all turned out well, the first thought of everyone was for the Queen!

Document B

SOURCE: **from a news article in** *The Guardian*, **March 2, 1900**

To describe with any degree of adequacy the excitement in London, and indeed throughout the country, consequent upon the announcement yesterday of the relief of Ladysmith would be an almost impossible task. The news was made known a few minutes before ten o'clock at the War Office, and soon after the hour the welcome intelligence was proclaimed by the Lord Mayor from a window of the Mansion House.

Document C

SOURCE: **H.W. Wilson, from** *With the Flag to Pretoria, A History of the Boer War, 1899–1900*, **1901**

The Boer scouts stealthily watched him, crawling through the thick bush in which a stranger without his bearings is as helpless as a ship without compass on the trackless ocean, and, on the information which they gave, Cronje marched swiftly north, and a second time placed himself on the British line of advance. Already runners had come in to the British camp from the north. One, from the brave and steadfast Colonel Plumer, announced that that officer would effect his junction with Mahon north-west of Mafeking; the other, from Colonel Baden-Powell, asked for information as to the numbers, guns, and supplies of the column.

Such information was not lightly to be entrusted to any messenger; there was no cipher of which Baden-Powell had the key; but in these straits, Colonel Rhodes, the intelligence officer with the column, succeeded in inventing a most ingenious reply, unintelligible to the Boers, but clear as daylight to the British. It is thus given by Mr. Filson Young: "Our numbers are the Naval and Military multiplied by ten; our guns, the number of sons in the Ward family; our supplies, the officer commanding the 9th Lancers." The key to the message was that there were 940 men, 94 Piccadilly being the number of the Naval and Military Club; that the guns were six, that being the number of sons in the house of Dudley; and that the supplies were little.

Document D

SOURCE: **from a news article in** *The Guardian*, **June 2, 1902**

The announcement of peace was made at the evening service at St. Paul's Cathedral to a fairly large congregation. . . . The Bishop of Stepney then ascended the pulpit and said: "I desire to announce to the congregation that God has been pleased to answer our prayers and to give us the blessings of peace." He added: "I will read to you the telegram which has been sent by the Commander-in-Chief to the Secretary of State for War." Having done this he proceeded: "Comment is needless, but I ask you to offer your heartfelt thanks to Almighty God by singing instead of the hymn on the paper another hymn suitable to the occasion, and to follow that by singing to the occasion, and to follow that by singing two verses of the National Anthem." The hymn referred to was "Now thank we all our God," and the congregation sang it with much feeling and impressiveness.

Document E

SOURCE: **Arthur Conan Doyle,** *The Great Boer War*, **1902**

Monday, October 30th, 1899, is not a date which can be looked back to with satisfaction by any Briton. In a scrambling and ill-managed action we had lost our detached left wing almost to a man, while our right had been hustled with no great loss but with some ignominy into Ladysmith. Our guns had been outshot, our infantry checked, and our cavalry paralysed. Eight hundred prisoners may seem no great loss when compared with a Sedan, or even with an Ulm; but such matters are comparative, and the force which laid down its arms at Nicholson's Nek is the largest British force which has surrendered since the days of our great grandfathers, when the egregious Duke of York commanded in Flanders.

Step 5 Part C—Analytical Transitions

Document F

> SOURCE: **L. S. Amery, *The Times History of the War in South Africa (1899–1902)*, 1902**
>
> The force Baden-Powell had with him was a mere handful—irregular mounted infantry, just learning to hold on to their saddles, Cape, Rhodesian, and Protectorate police, and a scratch selection of volunteers and town guard, with half-a-dozen antiquated little muzzleloaders for artillery—but animated with a spirit of confidence in themselves, and in the courage and resourcefulness of their leader, that was to prove of more worth than numbers or training, or batteries of field artillery, and to frustrate Cronje's hopes and the whole Boer plan of campaign in the west.

Document G

> SOURCE: **Sir Baden-Powell, from *Lessons from the Varsity of Life*, 1933**
>
> My orders were to raise two battalions of Mounted Rifles, to mount, equip, train, and supply them, with the least possible delay and the least possible display.
>
> … Also, I was to take charge of and organise the Police of Rhodesia and Bechuanaland as part of my force.
>
> But I was to make as little show as possible of these preparations for fear of precipitating war by arousing the animosity of the Boers.
>
> The object of my force and its establishment on the north-west border of the Transvaal was, in the event of war, to attract Boer forces away from the coast so that they should not interfere with the landing of British troops: secondly, to protect our possessions in Rhodesia and Mafeking, etc. Thirdly, to maintain British prestige among the great native tribes in those parts.

6. GLOBALIZATION EFFECTS ON WORLD SOCCER

Exercise Question: *Compare and contrast the effects of globalization on professional soccer clubs and World Cup national teams.*

7. IMPACT OF EUROPEAN DOMINANCE IN THE EARLY 20TH C.

Exercise Question: *Evaluate the extent to which the European dominance of the world at the beginning of the 20th century impacted the Middle East.*

6

Effective Closing Paragraphs

Directions: For the following exercises, practice all the skills covered so far in this book.

Step 1: Identify the tasks and terms

Step 2: Brainstorm specific evidence (analyze documents for DBQ)

Step 3: Develop a thesis and categories of evidence, and then outline your argument

Step 4: Write an opening paragraph

Step 5: Analyze your specific evidence in three body paragraphs and insert analytical transitions

Finally, write a closing paragraph for your essay. Remember that this final paragraph is your best opportunity to impress the reader and "stick the landing"! Summarize each part of your argument, alluding to your most significant evidence, and restate your thesis.

1. DEVELOPMENT OF THE RIVER VALLEY CIVILIZATIONS

Exercise Question: *Evaluate the extent to which there were similarities in the development of civilizations in the River Valleys.*

2. AGE OF EMPIRE IN THE CLASSICAL PERIOD

Exercise Question: To what extent should the political unity from 600 BCE to 600 CE in world history be regarded as an "Age of Empire"?

3. CENTRALIZATION IN THE INTER-REGIONAL PERIOD

Exercise Question: To what extent does the "Era of Centralization" accurately describe the global political systems from 600 CE to 1450 CE?

4. THE AGE OF REVOLUTIONS

Exercise Question: In what ways was the Taiping Rebellion in China similar to the Independence Revolutions in Latin America?

5. THE IMPACT OF TWENTIETH-CENTURY WARS

Exercise Question: Analyze the impact of twentieth-century wars on TWO of the following regions: Africa, Asia, Oceania, and South America.

6. ENVIRONMENTAL CHALLENGES OF THE 21ST CENTURY

Exercise Question: *Analyze the ways in which economic policy interacts with environmental policy in the 21st century.*

Document A

Source: **Stephen Harper, Canadian Prime Minister, remarks at the UN Climate Summit, September 25, 2007**

The core principle of Canada's approach to climate change is balance. ... We are balancing environmental protections with economic growth.

Document B

Source: **Ban Ki-moon, United Nations Secretary General, closing remarks at the UN Climate Summit, September 25, 2007**

We need to ensure that such an agreement is in force by 2012. ... undoubtedly there is a need for much deeper emission reductions from industrialized countries. ... The cost of inaction will far outweigh the cost of action. ... The current level of effort will not suffice.

Document C

> SOURCE: **Georg Kell, Executive Director, United Nations Global Compact, in an op-ed article entitled "Climate Change: Is Business Doing Enough?" February 23, 2009**
>
> …business must flex its advocacy muscle and push even more companies to take action on climate change—within their sectors, their markets, down their supply chains. Likewise, business should use its influence with policy makers to lobby for carbon reductions and workable technical standards. What we really need is [a] new era of business statesmanship driven by the realization that the time to act is now.

Document D

> SOURCE: **Yvo de Boer, United Nations Climate Chief, speaking with a newspaper about the need for a treaty from the international climate conference in Copenhagen, March 16, 2009**
>
> I get the impression talking to business people that they still want clarity from Copenhagen. If you're making investments now, for example in the energy sector, in power plants that are going to be around for the next 30 to 50 years, you can't really afford to keep waiting and waiting and waiting for governments to say where they're going to go on this issue.

Document E

> SOURCE: **Connie Hedegaard, Danish Minister for Climate and Energy, quote from a news interview, October 2, 2009**
>
> If the whole world comes to Copenhagen and leaves without making the needed political agreement, then I think it's a failure that is not just about climate. Then it's the whole global democratic system not being able to deliver results in one of the defining challenges of our century. And that is and should not be a possibility. It's not an option.

Document F

SOURCE: **News article entitled "The Czech Republic makes big money through carbon trading," October 2, 2009**

Under the Kyoto Protocol, the Czech Republic is committed to reducing its carbon emissions by eight percent from 1990 levels by 2012. ... So far, it has already cut them by 24 percent owing to industrial restructuring and other measures, giving the government 140 million units of carbon credits to sell...

Document G

SOURCE: **Yu Qingtai, Chinese climate envoy, quote from news interview, October 5, 2009**

In my view, the fundamental reason for a lack of progress is the lack of political will on the part of Annex 1 [industrialized] countries.

Multiple-Choice Questions

Questions 1–3 refer to the document that follows.

Some one may wonder why I go about in private giving advice and busying myself with the concerns of others, but not venture to come forward in public and advise the state. I will tell you why. You have heard me speak at sundry times For I am certain, O men of Athens, that if I had engaged in politics, I should have perished long ago, and done no good either to you or to myself. And do not be offended at my telling you the truth: for the truth is, that no man who goes to war with you or any other multitude, honestly striving against the many lawless and unrighteous deeds which are done in a state, will save his life; he who will fight for the right, if he would live even for a brief space, must have a private station and not a public one.

Socrates's Defense at His Trial, Recorded by Plato in **The Apology, c. 400 BCE**

1. A historian of fifth-century Greek society is most likely to use this source as evidence that

    a. Ancient Athens should be glorified as the birthplace of democracy

    b. Greek city-states relied heavily on elite judges to make laws

    c. Athenian democracy was not perfect in its administration of free speech

    d. Athens exploited Sparta in the Delian League against Persia

2. All of the following philosophers represent the ideals of the Greek sophists EXCEPT:

   a. Aristotle

   b. Plato

   c. Socrates

   d. Ashoka

3. Alexander the Great spread these sophist teachings marking the beginning of what era?

   a. Hellenistic Society (323 BCE)

   b. Polis Age (500 BCE)

   c. Punic Wars (264 BCE)

   d. Warring Period (403 BCE)

Questions 4–5 refer to the document that follows.

Island Capital of the Aztecs, Tenochtitlan (mural), Luis Covarrubias, (1919-1987) Museo Nacional de Antropologia, Mexico City, Mexico

4. Which of the following cannot be supported based on the image above?

   a. The Aztecs practiced a polytheistic belief system supported by the natural surroundings.

   b. The Aztecs had sophisticated engineering practices supported by the chinampas.

   c. The Aztecs established a thriving capital supported by the population size.

   d. The Aztecs practiced peaceful diplomacy with other natives as supported by the lack of walls.

5. Similar to Tenochtitlan, what urban center served a political and religious purpose in the Incan Empire?

   a. Tikal

   b. Cuzco

   c. Tula

   d. Aridoamerica

Question 6 refers to the document that follows.

I have had 13 children, and have brought seven up. I have been accustomed to work in the fields at hay-time and harvest. Sometimes I have had my mother, and sometimes my sister, to take care of the children, or I could not have gone out. I have gone to work at seven in the morning till six in the evening; in harvest sometimes much later, but it depends on circumstances. Women with a family cannot be ready so soon as men, and must be home earlier, and therefore they don't work so many hours.

Mrs. Smart, from an interview in Reports of Special
Assistant Poor Law Commissioners on the Employment
of Women and Children in Agriculture, London, 1843

6. Which of the following trends contributed most to the end of situations like that described in the document?

   a. factory labor laws restricting the number of hours worked in a day

   b. Victorian cultural norms that emphasized the domesticity of women

   c. poor laws aimed at caring for urban children in extreme poverty

   d. Suffragette movements that provided women with greater political power

Questions 7–8 refer to the document that follows.

The men who took commanding roles in the American Revolution were as unlikely a group of revolutionaries as one can imagine. Indeed to call them revolutionaries at all is almost ironic. With the possible (and doubtful) exception of Samuel Adams, none of those who took leading roles in the struggle actively set out to foment rebellion or found a republic. They became revolutionaries despite themselves.

Or rather, they became revolutionaries because a crisis in a single colony spiraled out of control in 1773-1774, and the empire's harsh response to the challenge to its authority persuaded colonists everywhere that the British government really was bent on abridging their basic rights and liberties. Until then, the men who soon occupied critical positions in the struggle for independence were preoccupied with private affairs and hopeful that the troubles that had roiled the empire in the 1760s would soon be forgotten. To catch them (as we repeatedly shall) at those moments when they individually realized that would not be the case is to understand that the Revolution made them as much as they made the Revolution.

Jack Rakove, **Revolutionaries: A New History of the Invention of America,** *2010*

7. In the paragraph, Rakove most clearly criticizes which of the following historical interpretations of the leaders of the American Revolution?

   a. America's revolutionary leaders were concerned with maintaining their plantation-based economic system.

   b. America's revolutionary leaders were driven, enlightened leaders with a desire for Independence.

   c. America's revolutionary leaders were replicating the actions of other colonists in Latin America.

   d. America's revolutionary leaders were patriotic farmers with no desire for revolution or change.

8. Based on your knowledge of the Latin American revolutions, which of the following creole leaders supports Rakove's argument as it relates to their revolution?

   a. Simon Bolivar

   b. Fidel Castro

   c. Juan Peron

   d. Che Guevara

Questions 9–10 refer to the document that follows.

India with her problems and struggles became just a part of this mighty world drama, of the great struggle of political and economic forces that was going on everywhere, nationally and internationally. In that struggle my own sympathies went increasingly toward the communist side. I had long been drawn to socialism and communism, and Russia had appealed to me. Much in Soviet Russia I dislike-the ruthless suppression of all contrary opinion, the wholesale regimentation, the unnecessary violence (as I thought) in carrying out various policies. But there was no lack of violence and suppression in the capitalist world, and I realized more and more how the very basis and foundation of our acquisitive society and property was violence. Without violence it could not continue for many days. A measure of political liberty meant little indeed when the fear of starvation was always compelling the vast majority of people everywhere to submit to the will of the few, to the greater glory and advantage of the latter. Violence was common in both places, but the violence of the capitalist order seemed inherent in it; while the violence of Russia, bad though it was aimed at a new order based on peace and cooperation and real freedom for the masses.

Jawaharlal Nehru, **Marxism, Capitalism**
and Non-Alignment, *1941*

9. Nehru's argument is best understood in the context of which of the following?

    a. Governments in Asia sought economic relief from the Industrial Revolution.

    b. Governments under the control of European colonizers sought independence.

    c. Governments in Europe successfully established democratic states in Asia.

    d. Governments under Mughal rule promoted a return to mercantilistic practices.

10. Which of the following developments would later undermine Nehru's commitment to communism and encourage participation in the non-alignment movement?

    a. Cold War

    b. World War II

    c. Vietnam War

    d. Globalization

Questions 11–12 refer to the document that follows.

… at a time when climate change climbs to the top of the political agenda, wind energy continues to be the only advanced technology ready and able to deliver renewable power on a large scale. Cyprus is not among the windiest areas in the world, yet still we have a commitment to go to renewable energy, so we have to work harder than others.

Akis Ellinas, chairman of DK Wind Supply,
quoted in Utility Week, October 5, 2009

11. Which of the following events is most closely associated with the document above?

    a. The Copenhagen Summit

    b. The Oslo Accord

    c. The Kyoto Protocol

    d. The SALT II Agreement

12. The argument of Akis Ellinas in the document above is most similar to which of the following?

    a. a British MP arguing for a law to reduce carbon emissions in the UK

    b. a University of Milan professor arguing for more solar power research

    c. a Volvo CEO arguing for a computerized solution to better MPG

    d. an army general arguing for a military solution to a border crisis in Croatia

Short-Answer Questions

1. Use the map below to answer both parts of the question that follows.

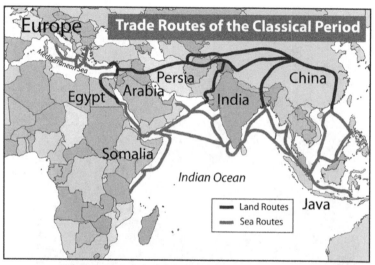

Trade Routes in the Classical Period, c. 100 BCE

(A) Briefly explain TWO effects on Eurasian economies during the classical period based on the trade network shown on the map above.

(B) Briefly explain ONE effect on Eurasian cultures during the classical period based on the trade network shown on the map above.

2. Answer both parts of the question.

   Should the urban centers that emerged from 600 CE to 1450 CE be classified as "Cosmopolitan Cities"?

   (A) Identify and explain TWO pieces of evidence that support the periodization above.

   (B) Identify and explain ONE piece of evidence that refutes the periodization above.

3. Use the illustration below to answer both parts of the question that follows.

(A) Briefly explain ONE economic development in the 16th and 17th centuries that gave rise to the crop production shown in the image above.

(B) Briefly explain TWO effects in the 16th – 18th centuries that emerged because of the crop production shown in the image above.

4. Use the excerpts to answer both parts of the question that follows.

There was then no sickness; they had no aching bones; they had then no high fever; they had then no smallpox; they had then no burning chest; they had then no abdominal pain; they had then no consumption; they had then no headache. At that time the course of humanity was orderly. The foreigners made it otherwise when they arrived here.

Anonymous aborigine of Yucatan, from an interview, speaking of pre-Spanish life, c. 1550

A Comanche on his feet is out of his element, and comparatively almost as awkward as a monkey on the ground, without a limb or a branch to cling to; but the moment he lays his hand upon his horse, his face even becomes handsome, and he gracefully flies away like a different being.

George Catlin, American painter, author, and traveler, 1841

(A) Briefly explain TWO economic developments that led to the situations shown in the two sources.

(B) Briefly explain ONE social development that led to the situations shown in the two sources.

5. Use the excerpts and your knowledge of world history to answer all parts of the question that follows.

...This habitual restraint produces a docility which woman requires all her life long, for she will always be in subjection to a man, or a man's judgment, and she will never be free to set her own opinion above his. What is most wanted in a woman is gentleness. ... A man, unless he is a perfect monster, will sooner or later yield to his wife's gentleness, and the victory will be hers.

Once it is demonstrated that men and women neither are, nor should be, constituted the same, either in character or in temperament, it follows that they should not have the same education. ... Boys want movement and noise, drums, tops, toy-carts; girls prefer things which appeal to the eye, and can be used for dressing-up-mirrors, jewelry, finery, and specially dolls ... The search for abstract and speculative truths for principles and axioms in science, for all that tends to wide generalizations, is beyond a woman's grasp.

Jean Jacques Rousseau, **Emile, or On Education,** *1762*

What opinion are we to form of a system of education, when the author (Rousseau in Emile) says... 'Educate women like men, and the more they resemble our sex the less power will they have over us.' This is the very point I am at. I do not wish them to have power over men, but over themselves. The most perfect education, in my opinion, is ... to enable the individual to attain such habits of virtue as will render it independent. In fact, it is a farce to call any being virtuous whose virtues do not result from the exercise of its own reason.

To be a good mother a woman must have sense, and that independence of mind which few women possess who are taught to depend entirely on their husbands. Meek wives are, in general, foolish mothers...

If children are to be educated to understand the true principle of patriotism, their mother must be a patriot ... make women rational creatures, and free citizens, and they will quickly become good wives, and mothers; that is-if men do not neglect the duties of husbands and fathers.

Mary Wollstonecraft, **A Vindication of the Rights of Women,** *1792*

(A) Briefly explain TWO political developments that led to the debate highlighted by the two sources.

(B) Briefly explain ONE social development that led to the debate highlighted by the two sources.

6. Use the excerpt to answer all parts of the question that follows.

As the people had not appeared for a single instant on the public stage for a hundred and forty years, the possibility of their ever appearing there was forgotten, and their insensibility was regarded as a proof of deafness. Hence, when some interest began to be taken in their lot, they were discussed publically as though they had not been present. It appeared as though it was supposed that the discussion would only be heard by the upper classes, and that the only danger was lest these might not be made to understand the case.

The very classes which had most to fear from public fury declaimed loudly and publically against the cruel injustice which the people had so long suffered ... Thus, in their endeavor to relieve the lower classes, they roused them to fury.

In the eighteenth century ... it was disinterested principle and generous sympathy which roused the upper classes to revolution, while the people were agitated by the bitter feeling of their grievances, and a rage to change their condition. The enthusiasm of the former fanned the flame of popular wrath and covetousness, and ended by arming the people.

Alexis de Tocqueville, **The Old Regime and the Revolution,** *1856*

(A) Provide ONE piece of evidence that supports Tocqueville's position.

(B) Provide ONE piece of evidence that undermines Tocqueville's position.

(C) Identify ONE example of any other revolution which contrasts with the description above.

7. Answer all parts of the question.

   (A) Identify and explain ONE important similarity between the policies of absolute monarchs (1600–1800) and fascist leaders (1900–1950).

   (B) Identify and explain ONE important difference between the policies of absolute monarchs (1600–1800) and fascist leaders (1900–1950).

   (C) Identify and explain ONE important historical development in World History that could account for the difference in policy.

8. Use the excerpt and the image to answer all parts of the question that follows.

My Lord, in the case of Taylor, Ibbotson & Co. I took the evidence from the mouths of the boys themselves. They stated to me that they commenced working on Friday morning, the 27th of May last, at six A.M., and that, with the exception of meal hours and one hour at midnight extra, they did not cease working till four o'clock on Saturday evening, having been two days and a night thus engaged. Believing the case scarcely possible, I asked every boy the same questions, and from each received the same answers. I then went into the house to look at the time book, and in the presence of one of the masters, referred to the cruelty of the case, and stated that I should certainly punish it with all the severity in my power. Mr Rayner, the certificating surgeon of Bastile, was with me at the time.

Extract from a Factory Inspectors report,
British Parliamentary Papers No. 353, 1836

Photograph of workers in a factory, 1903

(A) Briefly identify and describe ONE cause of the situation described and pictured above.

(B) Briefly identify and describe ONE result of the situation described and pictured above.

(C) Briefly identify and describe a similar situation in ONE country other than England.

9. Use the excerpt to answer all parts of the question that follows.

Unlike the purges of 1933, during which opponents of collectivization and Ukrainizers had been purged, in 1937 Stalin decided to liquidate the entire leadership of the Ukrainian Soviet government and the CPU … By June 1938 the top seventeen ministers of the Ukrainian Soviet government were arrested and executed. The prime minister, Liubchenko, committed suicide. Almost the entire Central Committee and Politburo of Ukraine perished. An estimated 37% of the Communist party members in Ukraine - about 170,000 people - were purged. In the words of Nikita Khrushchev, Moscow's new viceroy in Kiev, the Ukrainian party "had been purged spotless." The NKVD slated for extermination entire categories of people, such as kulaks, priests, former members of anti-Bolshevik armies, those who had been abroad or had relatives abroad, and immigrants from Galicia; even average citizens perished in huge numbers. An indication of the vast scope of the Great Purge was the discovery, during the Second World War, in Vinnytsia, of a mass grave containing 10,000 bodies of residents of the region who were shot between 1937 and 1938.

Orest Subtelny, Ukraine: A History, 1993

(A) Briefly identify and describe ONE cause of the events described above.

(B) Briefly identify and describe ONE result of the events described above.

(C) Briefly identify and describe similar actions taken by ONE country other than Russia.

10. Use the excerpt and your knowledge of world history to answer all parts of the question that follows.

One factor in Thatcher's electoral victory had been her commitment to a reduction of immigration. In a population of 53 million whites, Britain had 1 million people of West Indian origin and an equal number of Asians. Conservatives claimed that British civilization was threatened; workers feared competition from the immigrants; and some immigrant communities had a high incidence of crime, family breakdown, illegitimacy, and disorder. An English nationalist to the core, Thatcher shared the uneasiness of many of her countrymen about pockets of poorly assimilated immigrants. The challenge was to prepare legislation that was undeniably racist without appearing to be racist.

The solution adopted was a new definition of British citizenship that sloughed off the long-standing claims of Commonwealth residents. The Nationality Act of 1981 defined British citizenship as something other than being a subject of the queen. Full British citizenship went to people who resided in Britain or were closely related to citizens. The eligibility of Commonwealth immigrants for citizenship was restricted to people who had one parent or grandparent born in the United Kingdom.

The Nationality Bill had considerable support in both parties: the Conservatives were strong nationalists, and Labour wanted to protect jobs and keep wages up. The bill was strongly opposed by immigrant groups and the churches. It faced opposition in the House of Lords, where the Archbishop of Canterbury was a prominent opponent. Passage of the Nationality Act terminated the right of millions of former imperial subjects to settle in Britain. Essentially, the question of Commonwealth immigration was settled. Thatcher had fulfilled her campaign promise.

Earl A. Reitan, The Thatcher Revolution: Margaret Thatcher, John Major, Tony Blair, and the Transformation of Modern Britain, *2002*

(A) Provide ONE piece of evidence that supports Reitan's position that the Nationality Bill of 1981 was essentially racist.

(B) Provide ONE piece of evidence that undermines Reitan's position that the Nationality Bill of 1981 was essentially racist.

(C) Identify ONE country other than Britain that took similar actions in response to immigration.

Part 2

Answers & Explanations

Step

2 (LEQ)

Brainstorming and Organizing Evidence

1. THE NEOLITHIC REVOLUTION

Exercise Question: *Analyze the extent to which the Neolithic Revolution served as a cause for the establishment of civilizations.*

Agriculture	Increased population density	Government - Laws of Ur - Code of Hammurabi
Surplus food	**Sedentary lifestyle** Trade	Specialized labor Defense of resources Artwork Increased exchange networks - ideas and collective learning

The Neolithic Revolution is characterized by humanity's transition from hunter/gatherer to farmer. Although agriculture provided surplus food, trade-offs included longer workdays, poorer nutrition, and shorter life expectancy. Surplus food, however, allowed for some people to stop farming and do other work – specializing labor. Additionally, farming required a sedentary lifestyle which allowed for the accumulation of more possessions and more children. As population grew and population density increased, there was a need for more formalized government and defense of resources. Sedentary life also meant limiting resources to those found locally, and this eventually leads to trade. Through trade and warfare, Neolithic exchange networks expanded and collective learning accelerated.

Example categories of evidence that might be used to answer this question:

Increased population density created a need for formalized governments

- Laws of Ur (ca. 2000 BCE)
- Code of Hammurabi (ca. 1750 BCE)

Surplus food led to divisions of labor and sedentary lifestyle

- Non-farming roles
- Defense of resources

Sedentary lifestyle necessitated trade to access non-local goods

- Trade
- Expanded exchange networks
- New ideas
- Accelerated collective learning

2. HORTICULTURE TO AGRICULTURE

Exercise Question: Analyze the extent to which the transition from horticulture to agriculture caused transformations in human organizations, gender roles, and culture.

Horticulture required knowledge of plants – traditionally role of women among hunter/gatherers

Agriculture required the use of animals for labor – hunter/gatherer men had experience with animals

Horticulture increased food supply incrementally – still required nomadic lifestyle and small groups

Agriculture increased food supply exponentially – supported larger sedentary groups

Horticulture allows leisure at all social levels – provides time for "democratic" art

Agriculture is labor intensive (only non-farming elites have leisure) – leads to "elite" art

Example categories of evidence that might be used to answer this question:

Increased group size changes ruling structures

- Small nomadic bands everyone knows everyone else

- Larger sedentary groups create anonymity and need for formalized governments

Use of animal labor changed gender roles

- Horticulture relied on deep understanding of plants (women)

- Control of animals for labor necessitated understanding of animals (men)

Art is common to both pre- and post-Agriculture, but nature of artists changed

- Horticulture produced "democratic" art

- Agriculture produced "elite" art

3. UNIVERSAL RELIGIONS IN THE CLASSICAL PERIOD

Exercise Question: *Analyze the reasons for the rapid expansion of universal religions across Eurasia in the classical period (600 BCE – 600 CE).*

Religion	Methods Used
Judaism	- Old Testament and Hebrew Scriptures - Codification of Law an Ten Commandments
Jainism	- Disciplined Order of Monks - Jain Scriptures
Vedic Religion (later known as Hinduism)	- Sanskrit Scriptures - Art and Architecture
Hinduism	- Texts like Bhagavad Gita - Validating the Caste System
Buddhism	- Sutra and Other Scriptures - Optimistic Message - Establishment of Schools - Adaptability - Missionaries – Monks - Art and Architecture
Confucianism	- Confucius Writings like the Analects - Confucian Followers like Mencius and Xunzi - Rituals
Daoist	- Texts like Laozi - Poetry
Christianity	- New Testament - Missionaries - Art and Architecture

The belief systems of the classical period share many similarities in methods used to spread religious traditions and truths such as use of missionaries and reliance on written texts. For instance, many of these belief systems use texts to share beliefs, as seen in Judaism, Christianity, and Confucianism. The use of the written word allowed these beliefs systems to be recorded and shared as in the case of the Sutra in Buddhism. In addition, many of these classical period belief systems relied on missionaries and monks to spread their beliefs as seen in Jainism, Buddhism, Confucianism, and Christianity. Buddhist monks and Christian missionaries moved throughout Eurasia spreading their beliefs systems.

Example categories of evidence that might be used to answer this question:

Use of the Written Texts
- Judaism – Old Testament and Ten Commandments
- Hinduism – Bhagavad
- Buddhism – Sutra
- Confucianism – The Analects
- Daoism – Laozi
- Christianity – New Testament

Disciples and Followers
- Buddhist Monks
- Confucian Followers Mencius and Xunzi
- Christian Disciples like Matthew and Mark

Validating the Political System
- Hinduism – justifies the caste system
- Confucianism – supports the dynastic system
- Judaism – provides a clear code of ethics

4. GROWTH OF TRADING CITIES

Exercise Question: Compare and contrast the reasons for the growth of trading cities in different parts of the world from 600 CE to 1450 CE.

Trading City	Reasons for Growth
Baghdad	- Rise of a cosmopolitan city in the Abbasid Caliphate - Importance as a religious city in Islam - Large slave markets - Access to established trade routes on the Silk Road
Cordoba	- Rise of a cosmopolitan city in the Muslim world - University center with madrasas
Timbuktu	- Rise of a cosmopolitan city in the West African Kingdoms - Access to valuable raw materials – Gold and Salt - University center for Islam - Access to established trade routes in Sub-Saharan Africa
Kilwa	- Rise of a City-State - Natural Defenses - Access to established trade routes on the Indian Ocean - Access to Bantu (Interior of Africa)
Karakorum	- Rise of a cosmopolitan city in the Mongolian Empire - A political center in the Mongolian Empire - Assimilation of good economic practices

Trading City	Reasons for Growth
Venice	- Rise of a City-State - Economic increase because of war (i.e. Crusades) - Access to established trade routes on the Mediterranean Sea
Tenochtitlan	- Rise of a cosmopolitan city in the Aztec Empire - A political center in the Aztec Empire

Trading cities developed in the period 600 CE to 1450 CE for a series of reasons related to luxury items, technological innovation, and empire building. Because of the innovations in shipbuilding and sailing technology, more and more civilizations expanded their access to sea trade allowing for trading cities to grow. For example, the use of dhows, junks, and caravels improved access to sea trade in Europe, Africa, and Asia. In this era, the emergence of centralizing empires in the case of the Mongols and Abbasid Caliphate created the need for cosmopolitan centers; while other parts of the world relied on small local government in city states causing the growth of trading centers as seen in Venice and Kilwa. Nevertheless, many of the expanding trading cities grew on existing trade routes. Prior to this era, trade routes such as the Silk Road and Sub-Saharan Trade Route were already established providing cities like Baghdad and Timbuktu a foundation to grow.

Example categories of evidence that might be used to answer this question:

Access to Demanded Luxury Items

- Silks
- Porcelain
- Gold
- Salt
- Slaves

Use of Existing Trade Routes

- Silk Road
- Mediterranean Sea
- Trans-Saharan Trade Route
- Indian Ocean Trade Route

Technological Improvements

- Ships (Dhows)
- Compass
- Astrolabe

City-States

- Tenochtitlan in the Aztec Empire
- Venice in Italy

Rise of Cosmopolitan, Political Centers

- Abbasid City of Baghdad
- West African City of Timbuktu
- Mongolian City of Khartoum

Importance of University Centers

- Cordoba
- Timbuktu
- Baghdad

5. ISLAMIC KINGDOMS

Exercise Question: Compare and contrast the key characteristics of the two primary Islamic kingdoms of the 16th century, the Ottomans and the Safavids.

Ottomans	Safavids
Gained power from decline of Mongols in Anatolia	Gained power from decline of Mongols in Persia
Suleiman the Magnificent	Persian empire
Selim	Shia Islam
Suleymaniye Mosque	Ismail
Topkapi Palace	Tabriz
Sunni Islam	Centralized governance
Multilingual kingdom	Shah
	cont'd

Ottomans	Safavids
Flexible administration of conquered territories	Intolerant of diversity
	"Shiism or death"
Decentralized governance and tax collection	
Janissaries	
Expansive empire	
Istanbul	

Example categories of evidence that might be used to answer this question:

Comparable origins

- Both gained power (pre-1500) as a result of Mongol decline

- Both originally small Islamic groups with little power

Contrasting governing styles

- Ottomans allowed local governance (constrained only by imperial loyalty and tax collection)

- Safavids governed all territories centrally from Tabriz

- Ottoman flexibility permitted a large empire

- Safavid centralization limited the size of the empire

Contrasting cultures

- Ottomans were Sunni Muslims

- Safavids were Shia Muslims

- Ottoman empire was multilingual (reflecting local administration)

- Safavids enforced the language of Persia
- Ottomans were tolerant of all religions within the empire
- Safavids required "Shiism or death"

6. INDUSTRIALIZATION OF JAPAN AND BRITAIN

Exercise Question: *Compare and contrast the process of industrialization in Japan with the earlier industrialization of Britain.*

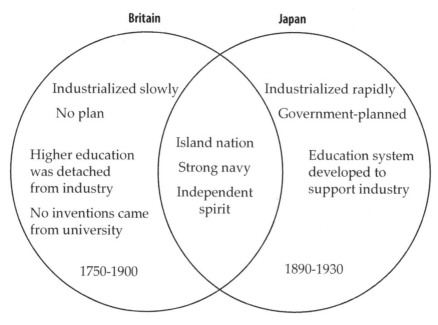

Britain   **Japan**

Industrialized slowly   Industrialized rapidly

No plan   Government-planned

Island nation

Higher education was detached from industry   Strong navy   Education system developed to support industry

No inventions came from university   Independent spirit

1750-1900   1890-1930

Example categories of evidence that might be used to answer this question:

Both island nations

- Strong naval presence
- Independent spirit

Speed of industrialization was very different

- Britain was first to industrialize in world (1750)
- Britain continued gradual industrialization for 150 years
- Japan began industrialization very late (1890)
- Japan industrialized very quickly (40 years)

Path of industrialization was very different

- Britain's industrialization was haphazard (no plan)
- British schools played no role in innovation or industrialization (university was "elite")
- Japan's industrialization was methodical and controlled by the Meiji government
- Japan reorganized its public education system to support innovation and industrialization

7. INTERWAR ART

Exercise Question: To what extent was Interwar Art unique from art of the period immediately before World War I?

Irrationalism	Surrealism
- Friedrich Nietzsche	- Salvador Dali
- Fyodor Dostoevsky	- Max Ernst
- Henri Bergson	- Pablo Picasso
- Georges Sorel	
- Dante Gabriel Rossetti	
- Oscar Wilde	
- Dadaism	

Postwar Artistic Technique
- Use of color based in earlier palettes (Franz Marc)
- Postwar artists were students of prior artists
- Some postwar artists worked through war (Modigliani)

Example categories of evidence that might be used to answer this question:

Postwar artists imitated colors and styles of earlier artists (not unique)
- Franz Marc
- Picasso
- Surrealism
- Friedrich Nietzsche
- Fyodor Dostoevsky

Postwar artists included some whose work predates the war (not unique)
- Modigliani
- Picasso
- Ernst

Surrealist art was, at least partially, reaction to the war (unique)
- Dali
- Ernst
- Picasso

8. WWII CONFERENCES AND COLD WAR POLICY

Exercise Question: *Analyze the impact of WWII Allied conferences on subsequent Cold War policy.*

Allied Conferences

- Washington (Churchill, FDR)
- Casablanca (Churchill, FDR, de Gaulle)
- Cairo (Churchill, FDR, Chiang Kai-shek)
- Teheran (Churchill, FDR, Stalin)
- San Francisco (UN)
- Malta (Churchill, FDR)
- Yalta (Churchill, FDR, Stalin)
- Potsdam (Churchill, Attlee, Truman, Stalin)

Major Players

- Churchill
- FDR
- Stalin
- Truman
- Chiang Kai-shek

Cold War Policies/ Organizations

- NATO
- SEATO
- Warsaw Pact
- Buffer states
- Berlin Wall
- Mutually Assured Destruction
- United Nations

Example categories of evidence that might be used to answer this question:

Exclusion of Soviets from early Allied conferences

- Washington
- Casablanca
- Cairo

Animosity between Stalin and Churchill

- Stalin
- Churchill

American diplomacy isolated Soviets

- San Francisco
- UN
- NATO
- SEATO

Step 2 (DBQ)

Using the 3-Step Process to Analyze Documents for the DBQ

1. JEWISH DIASPORA IN THE CLASSICAL PERIOD

Exercise Question: In what ways did the Jewish diaspora of the classical period impact the bond amongst the followers of Judaism?

Document A

SUMMARIZE – The Ten Commandments provide a list of rules to be followed by Jews. The list includes religious practices like following only one God and keeping the Sabbath. In addition, the Ten Commandments provide a code of ethics such as not stealing, committing murder, or lying.

ANALYZE – While the list had been passed down by word of mouth, the Jewish Diaspora may have caused these rules to be written down in the 6th century BCE to ensure consistency across the Middle East, Africa, and Europe. The Jewish Diaspora created a need for a clear list of rules ensuring a common bond amongst Jews in the classical period.

CRITICIZE – Since this is a religious list of laws, the purpose of the document was to clearly articulate the most important rules for its followers. Since the laws were recorded after being passed down by word of mouth, it is important to note that some of the language may have changed over the centuries.

Document B

SUMMARIZE – The Book of Kings describes the manner in which the king of Assyria used his army to attack and conquer Jerusalem. The source notes that the king of Assyria brought a "great army" against the Jewish territory. According to the source, the Assyrian military attacked because the Jews rebelled first as noted in the line "that you rebel against me".

ANALYZE – Through resistance, rebellion, and warfare, the Jewish diaspora created a common bond as Jews attempted to resist expanding empires like the Assyrians and maintain their homeland.

CRITICIZE – Jeremiah was a Hebrew (Jewish) prophet so he may have exaggerated the Assyrian threat to help consolidate the Jewish identity in the 6th century BCE. Since this text was included in the Old Testament, we can assume that its message was important to the Jewish people.

Document C

SUMMARIZE – The Sanhedrin provides another list of rules for Jews to follow in the classical period. Jewish cities must have a series of specific characteristics: a court of law, a synagogue, a bath house, and a bathroom. Moreover, teachers, doctors, and craftsmen must be available within the city.

ANALYZE – The document provides another list of rules for Jews. These laws were passed by a court of Jewish judges to ensure the maintenance of religious practices via the building of synagogues and schools as well as the establishment of craftsmen and doctors to create a sense of community. If the followers of Judaism adhered to these laws, they would ensure some cultural uniformity in an era of great mobility.

CRITICIZE – Since this set of laws was written around 50 BCE, it coincides with one of the largest diasporas in history. It seems reasonable to assume that Jewish leaders wanted to reinforce the rules of uniformity at a time when so many of their followers were on the move.

Document D

SUMMARIZE – *The War of the Jews* describes the manner in which the Romans conquered a Jewish territory. The document describes the bloodlust of the Roman army as they conquered the Jewish territory, "slew" the Jews "without mercy," and set fire to the city.

ANALYZE – Similar to Document B, this source demonstrates the hardships experienced by Jews as they resisted expanding empires. In this case, the Jewish Diaspora created a common bond as Jews experienced hardship under Roman rule.

CRITICIZE – Josephus was a Judeo-Roman scholar providing a firsthand account of the wars against Jews in the Roman Empire. Since the author is a historian, it can be assumed that he is attempting to convey the the story as he understood it. Because he had experience in both Judeo and Roman histories, he would be able to understand the context and his perspective might be somewhat less one-sided. Of course, since Josephus was writing this book at the request of the Roman emperor, he may have been compelled to show the Roman army in a more positive light.

Document E

SUMMARIZE – The relief shows the siege of Jerusalem as the Romans take valuables from the Jews. In the relief, the Romans carry religious artifacts as well as people's personal property.

ANALYZE – Similar to Documents B and D, this source demonstrates the hardships experienced by Jews as expanding empires conquered their territory. The looting of Jewish synagogues and homes created a common bond as Jews experienced hardship under Roman rule.

CRITICIZE – This is a relief on the Arch of Titus. The Romans constructed arches to honor great men and great victories. Therefore, the purpose of this relief was to honor the actions of the Roman military. The artist may have exaggerated the extent of the looting in order to boost the reputation of Titus within Rome.

Document F

SUMMARIZE – The Greek Inscription recognizes the role of Theodotos and his family in the building and maintaining of a synagogue in Jerusalem. The synagogue in Jerusalem was used to teach the Torah and commandments as well as provide respite for travelers.

ANALYZE – This source recognizes the emerging role of synagogues in the classical period as places of worship. Synagogues allowed Jews to come together and create a community. Moreover, because of the

Jewish Diaspora, synagogues also provided lodging for travelers. In combination with Document C, we can see that every Jewish city provided an opportunity for travelers to remain connected to the larger Jewish community.

CRITICIZE – This is an inscription on a synagogue so it may have been intended as information about the purpose of the structure within the city of Jerusalem. Since it was written in Greek, its intended audience may have included non-Jews who would have been unfamiliar with the Hebrew language.

Document G

SUMMARIZE – This is a map showing the Jewish Diaspora in the classical period. Arrows indicate the movement of people from Jerusalem into parts of Africa, the Middle East, and Asia, showing the extent of Jewish mobility.

ANALYZE – The map demonstrates the vast territory in which Jews traveled and settled in the classical period. Because of the mass migration, there emerged a need for places of worship, written text, and common laws to be followed by all Jews.

CRITICIZE – Since this map has been created by modern historians, it can be viewed as a visual summary of specific historical records (censuses, genealogies, etc.).

Outside Evidence:

- Babylonian Captivity – A period of exile for Jews starting in the 6th century BCE

- Assyria – a military monarchy which relied on tributes to maintain power

- Talmud – another body of Jewish laws contained in the Mishnah and Gemara

- Hellenistic Culture – the impact of Alexander the Great on the Jewish peoples

- Jewish slavery in the Roman Empire

Possible Categories of Evidence:

- Establishment of a Clear Code of Laws: A, C

- Creation of Synagogues: C, F

- Creation of Urban Centers: C, F, G

- Hardship: B, D, E

- Resistance: B, D

2. EFFECTS OF THE WEST AFRICAN KINGDOMS

Exercise Question: Analyze the cross-cultural effects of trade with the Western African Kingdoms in the Medieval Period (900 CE–1550 CE).

Document A

SUMMARIZE – The map of trade routes intersecting with West Africa illustrates the extent to which trade occurred across North Africa and East Africa. The map also denotes routes used for the slave trade in the Medieval Age. In addition, the map also identifies empires and civilizations like Ethiopia, Ghana, and Zimbabwe by name.

ANALYZE – The map demonstrates the extent of the cross-cultural impact of the West African Kingdoms on North and East African civilizations. The trade routes allowed for exchange of goods and ideas among numerous civilizations as clear routes emerged in this period. Moreover, the map illustrates the pervasive nature of the slave trade.

CRITICIZE – Since this is a modern map generated to illustrate medieval trade routes in Africa as well as the slave trade, it can be considered a reliable source.

Document B

SUMMARIZE – "The Description of Africa" addresses the city of Timbuktu in West Africa. The author recognizes the number of merchants and shops in Timbuktu. In addition, Joannes Leo Africanus notes the various goods available for trade such as European fabrics, grains, milk, and animals. While many items were widely available, salt was in short supply.

ANALYZE – The cross-cultural exchange of goods flourished as items were exchanged with places as far as Europe creating great wealth in trading centers like Timbuktu. This source provides a clear list of goods. Since the author is Spanish, it demonstrates the curiosity of Europeans regarding this trade route.

CRITICIZE – Joannes Leo Africanus provides a unique point of view as a Spanish Muslim. As a Spaniard, he is an outsider describing the city; yet, as a Muslim, he shares a common belief system with the city's residents. Since the format of this is a published book, Leo Africanus intended for his description to be read by a European audience. His praiseworthy language denotes a sense of amazement in the wealth of Timbuktu.

Document C

SUMMARIZE – "Rihla" provides an account of the city of Timbuktu. In particular, Ibn Battuta notes the European fabrics used by the leader. He also identifies the wealth of the leader by addressing the gold and silver as well as the numerous instruments. The city of Timbuktu had clear laws allowing for trade to flourish. Moreover, the document alludes to the impact of Islam in West Africa.

ANALYZE – The document provides another example of the growing wealth in Timbuktu and, by noting "European fabrics," highlights the exchange of resources with Europe. This is the first source to recognize the diffusion of Islam via trade centers.

CRITICIZE – The "Rihla" is a personal account of the city of Timbuktu written three years after visiting the city. Because of the length of time, Ibn Battuta may have forgotten certain facts or misrepresented some information. Similar to Leo Africanus, he is a Muslim and shares a similar belief system. The audience of this source is other Muslims across North Africa.

Document D

SUMMARIZE – The Catalan Atlas provides an illustration of trade within West Africa. The merchants travel on camels along the trade routes. The illustration shows urban centers and strong regional leaders. Mosques are scattered throughout the map.

ANALYZE – Similar to source A, this source demonstrates the extent of the trade networks in West Africa. Merchants travel to numerous cities exchanging goods and ideas. In particular, the cross-cultural diffusion of Islam is clearly demonstrated by the number of mosques. Again, since the map is from Spain, it demonstrates the curiosity of Europeans to know more about West Africa because it served as a major trading hub.

CRITICIZE – This contemporary map was produced by a Spanish cartography school which may demonstrate a European interest in West African kingdoms. The fact that it was produced by cartographers may mean that it is relatively reliable and accurate for its time.

Document E

SUMMARIZE – The personal account demonstrates the importance of Ghana as a trading post as gold and salt are heavily taxed going in and out of the region. The source identifies the carrying of gold "all over the place" showing the extent of trade.

ANALYZE – Similar to source B, this source demonstrates the goods being exchanged throughout West Africa. The source stresses the importance of the gold and salt trade.

CRITICIZE – Similar to Document B, Al-Bakir provides the point of view of a Spanish Muslim. As a Spaniard, he is an outsider describing the city; yet, as a Muslim, he shares a common belief system with the city's residents. Since the format of this source is a personal account, Al-Bakir may not have intended for the text to be read, making it a more reliable account.

Document F

SUMMARIZE – This manuscript is written in Arabic. The three circles on these pages are each divided into 12 parts. In addition to goods, the trade routes in West Africa shared language, ideas, and literature.

ANALYZE – This source recognizes the cross-cultural exchange of ideas. Arabic served as a universal language allowing ideas related to Islam as well as literature and mathematics to be exchanged. The 12-part circles may be connected to time and the calendar. This source re-enforces the importance of Islam as seen in Documents C and D.

CRITICIZE – This document is a copy of an Arabic text from the medieval period. It likely provides excellent insights into Arabic thought—if you can read medieval Arabic script.

Document G

SUMMARIZE – This document examines the trading city of Timbuktu and notes the riches acquired from West Africa via camel caravans. In particular, the goods mentioned are brass, silver, gold, pepper and slaves. The source also notes the dominance of the religion of Islam in the region.

ANALYZE – This source recognizes the impact of cross-cultural exchange on ideas. The source complements the importance of the diffusion of Islam as seen in Documents C, D, and F. Moreover, it complements Documents B and E by articulating the exchange of goods. Thus, cross-regional diffusion occurred in North Africa via the camel caravan.

CRITICIZE – This document is an explorer's personal account of trade along the African coast. Since he is an explorer and slave trader, he has significant knowledge of trade in this region and probably kept honest records in order to ensure future economic success. Moreover, since this is a personal account, he may not have intended the information to be shared.

Outside Evidence:

- Middle Passage – The movement of slaves from Africa to the Americas in the Age of Exploration

- Mansa Musa – a leader of the Mali who prospered from the trade routes

- Henry the Navigator – A Portuguese Prince interested in sea exploration and trade with West Africa

- Hajj – the pilgrimage to Mecca taken by a Muslim at least once

- Moor – a Spanish Muslim during the Medieval Period

Possible Categories of Evidence:

- Escalation of the Slave Trade: A, C

- Import and Export of Goods: B, D, G

- Demand for Luxury Goods: B, C, D

- Diffusion of Islam: C, D, F, G

- Exchange of Language and Literature: F

3. EXPANSION OF LANDED EMPIRES

Exercise Question: Analyze the causes of the expansion of landed empires from 1450 to 1750.

Document A

SUMMARIZE – The Portrait of Peter the Great illustrates the growing power of centralized monarchs in this time period. Peter the Great is depicted in a fur cape and armor with a naval vessel in the background. On the table, Peter's crown is resting.

ANALYZE – Peter the Great is depicted in a powerful disposition. He stands tall and proud as a strong leader. Moreover, the armor and naval vessel denote the growing power of the Russian military. For this landed empire, the need to acquire a warm water port became essential in order to increase Russia's territory, economy, and presence in Eastern Europe.

CRITICIZE – Since this royal portrait was produced by a British portrait painter, it provides a unique perspective. The painter has experience displaying the grandeur of monarchs which may make Peter appear stronger than in reality. However, this portrait painter has no allegiance to the Russian royal family and may be painting the Russian monarch as he is.

Document B

SUMMARIZE – *The History of Peter the Great* provides an account of Peter the Great's military. The source describes the construction of a new city to defend against the Swedes. In particular, the source notes details related to the foundation and walls. This new fortification provides the Russian military with water access via the Baltic Sea.

ANALYZE – This source supports the growing power of the Russian military under Peter the Great. The Russian tsar is improving the strength of the military by building new and more secure fortifications as well as gaining access to ports. In this particular source, Gordon notes the need for military strength in the northwest territory in order to protect against Swedish threats.

CRITICIZE – Alexander Gordon possessed a first-hand view of the growing power of the Russian monarch. As a member and leader of the military, he would have first-hand knowledge of the changes implemented by Peter the Great. Since this was a published book, Gordon may be protecting his career and legacy by speaking in a more positive manner.

Document C

SUMMARIZE – "An Account of India and the Great Moghul" provides a description of the Mughal Empire in India. The source notes the vast size of this landed empire as well as the system by which it maintains control of regional powers. The empire maintains control and expands its territory by forcing regional leaders to perform services and by creating division amongst the regional powers.

ANALYZE – The document provides different methods by which this landed empire expanded and maintained control of its territory. For the Mughals, they manipulated the local regional leaders in order acquire tribute and increase their wealth. Moreover, regional leaders could provide military assistance to boost the strength of the empire.

CRITICIZE – This account was written by a Frenchman who visited India for 12 years and served in the Mughal court. Since he resided in the empire for a long time and served in the court, his account was probably more accurate and factual. Nevertheless, as a foreigner, he may have misunderstood local customs and traditions.

Document D

SUMMARIZE – The Turkish Letters describes the military of the Ottoman Empire. In particular, the source gives a detailed description of the Janissary as well as campaign strategies. While on campaign, mules and camels are used to transport supplies. In the Ottoman military, men are appointed based on merit rather than rank or title.

ANALYZE – Similar to source B, this source demonstrates the military expertise of a landed empire. Instead of fortifications, the Ottoman Empire relies on a strategic transportation system to move food and supplies to the battlefield. Yet, this source also notes the reliance on the Janissary, the royal guard. Unlike the Mughals, this fighting force is loyal to the centralized leader.

CRITICIZE – Ogier Ghiselin de Busbecq was a Dutch Ambassador to the Ottoman Empire. As a European living in the empire, he would have witnessed and observed the power of the military. Moreover, since these were private letters written to his native country, he was most likely trying to accurately inform his leader of the military prowess of the Ottoman Empire.

Document E

SUMMARIZE – The report describes the diplomatic and military knowledge of Shah Abbas I, the leader of the Safavid Empire in the Middle East. This account notes Shah Abbas I implemented military reform by creating the office of commander-in-chief, installing a draft, and relying on muskets. In addition, Shah Abbas I researched his neighboring countries in order to be prepared.

ANALYZE – Similar to source B and D, this source demonstrates the need for a strong military in order to maintain and expand the empire. For Shah Abbas I, he implemented reforms to improve the condition and expertise of his army. Similar to source A, Shah Abbas I possesses a military presence in his empire.

CRITICIZE – This source was written by Father Simon and Vincent as a report to the Pope in Europe. Since this report was intended to inform the Pope on the status of Shah Abbas I, it can be assumed the authors were providing factual details in an attempt to accurately report on the military prowess of the Safavid Empire.

Document F

SUMMARIZE – The painting of the Shah Jahan demonstrates the presence of the leader of the Mughal Empire. The Shah is shown in fine clothing riding a horse in a proud body-position. His demeanor and disposition is one of power and prestige.

ANALYZE – Similar to source A, this leader demonstrates his strength by creating a royal portrait in which he demonstrates his power by his posture and wealth. The ability to produce visual pieces of propaganda aided in the ability of empires to show power through wealth and appearances.

CRITICIZE – Like source A, this was produced by a court painter; therefore, Payag may be exaggerating the appearance, posture and wealth of Shah Jahan. Payag was a noted portrait painter for multiple Mughal Emperors which demonstrates his ability to please the royal family through his grand depictions.

Document G

SUMMARIZE – The Articles of Agreement between the Cossacks and the Russian tsar provides a clear example of how landed empires increased the size of their military by relying on foreigners and regional powers. In particular, because the Cossacks possessed military skills, the Russian leader willingly provided the Cossacks select rights in order to win their support.

ANALYZE – Similar to Documents C and D, this source shows the need to create a larger standing army. Like Document C, the Russian tsar relied on outsiders. The Cossacks sought rights in order to agree to serve in the Russian military.

CRITICIZE – Since this was a signed agreement between two parties, the document may be a more reliable source. It would probably have been difficult for either side to skew the facts as they were understood at the time, though we have no way of knowing if both parties intended to abide by the agreement.

Outside Evidence:

- Ottoman Empire – An empire that demonstrated its expansionist policies with Osman I

- Constantinople/Istanbul – The conquest of the Byzantine Empire by the Ottoman Empire

- Akbar I – a leader of the Mughal Empire that unified northern India

- Gunpowder Empires – empires that relied on gunpowder to strengthen their military

Possible Categories of Evidence:

- Strong Leaders: A, E, F

- Size of the Military/Recruitment: C, D, E, G

- Military Reform: A, B, E

- Cunning Leadership: C, E, G

- Fortification: A

- Intelligence Gathering: E

4. STABILITY OF THE MUGHAL EMPIRE

Exercise Question: *Analyze the stability of the Mughal Empire between 1504 and 1858.*

Document A

SUMMARIZE – Babur recounts the events of late December 1523 on his approach to Lahore. He says that he sent two envoys to Lahore to encourage their chiefs (begs) to join him rather than oppose him in battle. He confirms that he has heard that two of Lahore's chiefs are prepared to fight, but he believes that gathering allies prior to his attack is worth the wait.

ANALYZE – His decision to pause and wait for a response from the begs of Lahore may be evidence of Babur's confidence and control in battle, and the tone of the passage reinforces this view. If this sort of circumspection extends to his governing style, Babur's rule over India may have been reasoned and even-handed, rather than ideological and iron-fisted.

CRITICIZE – The Babur-nama is at least partially autobiographical and written in retrospect, so the rationale for Babur's various decisions might have been embellished to enhance the great king's reputation.

Document B

SUMMARIZE – Hasan writes that every locality in the Mughal empire was protected by a kotwal who enforced social and economic norms. He implies, though it is not stated outright in the excerpt, that the kotwal is a local resident, and certainly his assistants are local residents.

ANALYZE – The fact of the kotwali serves as evidence of two important features of Mughal rule: imperial tolerance of local customs and norms, and local control over the enforcement of those customs and norms. If these officials existed as early as Babur's reign, this seems to add credence to the notion that he was not guided primarily by ideology.

CRITICIZE – The document comes from a history scholar in a published book. Professor Hasan is, in fact, working in India, but we should assume that his published works have passed the same sort of peer-review muster as would those of any other history scholar around the world. Because this book was published in 2006, it benefits from global research into the 21st century. Hasan may have a particular academic bias, but we have no way to know what it might be.

Document C

SUMMARIZE – Farooqui describes the general open-mindedness of Akbar – even from an early age. The excerpt goes on to detail the progression of Akbar's royal acts that gradually loosened restrictions on non-Muslims in India.

ANALYZE – The document is evidence of Akbar's inclusive governing style. If we assume that autonomy and stability go hand in hand, then Akbar's empire must have been relatively stable.

CRITICIZE – Like the previous document, this excerpt comes from an historical monograph written by a professional history scholar. Since we know little else about this author or his book, we must assume once again that the work has been subjected to professional scrutiny during the publication process, so it is likely a reliable and (perhaps) even-handed summary of Akbar and his governance.

Document D

SUMMARIZE – Richards traces a series of events that occurred at the start of Jahangir's reign. He implies several cause and effect relationships and uses language (eg., "irksome") that implies some knowledge of the emperor's interior motivations.

ANALYZE – The evidence in this document seems to support the notion that Jahangir changed the direction of the Mughal government's approach to non-Muslim Indians. It also suggests that his reasons included a need for greater control over defiant Rajputs. If this is true, the document might be used to counter the notion of stability through autonomy, and it certainly will support the conclusion that Mughal rule became less tolerant under Jahangir.

CRITICIZE – Like Farooqui and Hasan, Richards is a professional history scholar and the document is excerpted from a published book. Richards' description, however, is more narrative and, therefore, relies heavily on cause-and-effect relationships among the events listed. While there is nothing inherently wrong (or suspicious) about this writing style, and, as with the other scholarly works, we can assume this passed muster with his peers; it is also possible that some of them might have drawn other conclusions. In the absence of any competing views, however, we will have to assume that this work is relatively reliable.

Document E

SUMMARIZE – Emperor Aurangzeb's General Order calls for the destruction of all Hindu temples and schools and the silencing of all Hindu teachings.

ANALYZE – This document shows a clear break with the religious tolerance of Akbar just over a hundred years earlier, as evidenced in Document C. In conjunction with Document D, we have evidence that the empire's views toward its non-Muslim subjects has shifted from religious tolerance and political autonomy to intolerance and restriction.

CRITICIZE – Aside from the translation, we have here the actual words of the Order, so reliability should be assumed. You might also note from the tone of the Order that Aurangzeb has used sharply religious language, perhaps to rally support from Islamic clerics within the empire.

Document F

SUMMARIZE – This royal order reestablishes the jizyah tax on non-Muslims, 115 years after Akbar had abolished it.

ANALYZE – This is another document that can support a Mughal move toward a less tolerant and more centrally controlled empire.

CRITICIZE – Like Document E, this represents the actual words of the emperor's order. It should be interpreted at face value.

Document G

SUMMARIZE – Abu Fazl describes Akbar's abolition of slavery in India in 1562. He also justifies the decision on moral grounds. Additionally, he writes that women and children will no longer be held to account for the actions of their husbands and fathers.

ANALYZE – This is more evidence of Akbar's open-mindedness and adherence to reason rather than ideology. He disallows a time-honored practice for no reason except that it is the right thing to do.

CRITICIZE – The Akbar-nama, like the Babur-nama, was written, at least in part, to memorialize the reign of the emperor. Additionally, the author is not simply commissioned by Akbar to write the book, but he is a personal friend of the emperor. For all of these reasons, we might assume that some of the language may be embellished to Akbar's advantage. That being said, the spirit of the content of this document is corroborated by at least one other document.

Outside Evidence:

Almost all history textbooks address the leadership styles of both Babur and Akbar, and those descriptions are likely to corroborate the documentary evidence here. Both leaders are often described as tolerant and open-minded. Akbar is remembered as Akbar the Great, and his reign is widely accepted as the height of the Mughal Empire. Although the empire lasted into the 1800s, it is generally seen as declining from the 1670s (after Aurangzeb).

Possible Categories of Evidence:

Religious Tolerance

- Babur was less interested in religion and administration than in military conquest – C, E, F

Local Autonomy

- Akbar the Great – B, C, D, F, G

Non-Muslim Opposition

- Increased after Aurangzeb – A, C, D, F

5. NAPOLEON IN EGYPT

Exercise Question: Discuss the impact of Napoleon on the culture and society of Egypt.

Document A

SUMMARIZE – al-Jabarti describes the good times in Egyptian society before Napoleon.

ANALYZE – The evidence may support an argument that Napoleon's impact on society was negative.

CRITICIZE – As an Egyptian, al-Jabarti may be influenced by a sense of national pride and, consequently, he may be expected to view Napoleon's conquest as a negative event in Egyptian history.

Document B

SUMMARIZE – Napoleon says that he opposes the Mameluke oppressors and supports the Muslims.

ANALYZE – This document could be used to support the contention that Egyptian society was improved by Napoleon's influence, or at least to counter the argument that life was good before Napoleon.

CRITICIZE – Since Napoleon's success in Egypt would benefit from support from the local population, he could be expected to distinguish French domination from Mameluke domination. Egyptian Muslims may be more easily won over if they viewed Napoleon as a kindred spirit.

Document C

SUMMARIZE – Napoleon says that the Mamelukes have no right to control Egypt, and they have kept all that is good in the country away from the people of Egypt.

ANALYZE – Again, the document implies that Napoleon will improve the society (and perhaps the culture) for the Egyptians by eliminating the Mamelukes.

CRITICIZE – Like Document B, Napoleon may have used this public proclamation to win support from the local population.

Document D

SUMMARIZE – Bourrienne writes of Napoleon's use of public execution to secure stability in Egypt.

ANALYZE – The document says little about society or culture, but may be used to support an argument about Napoleon's methods.

CRITICIZE – It is possible that Bourrienne embellishes the situation a bit to make himself sound more humane in retrospect—30 plus years after the fact. Napoleon's ultimate fate may also give cause for Bourrienne to look more humane in his memoirs.

Document E

SUMMARIZE – Bourrienne writes that Napoleon intended to stay in Egypt to colonize it and introduce new cultural benefits.

ANALYZE – The evidence again speaks to Napoleon's motives and also serves to support the intention of cultural improvement.

CRITICIZE – Note comments for Document D. It should also be noted that any memoir written 30 years later, no matter which way the political winds blow, could be skewed by the writer's memory.

Document F

SUMMARIZE – St. John describes the effectiveness of Egyptian military training in the late-19th or early-20th century.

ANALYZE – Although the document is well outside the range of dates in this essay, it might help to support an argument that Egyptian society and culture were better after Napoleon.

CRITICIZE – If St. John is a casual observer (there is no evidence to counter that view), one could argue that his observations might be objective. One issue with this document is that it gives no indication of the date of St. John's visit, so the accuracy of his recollection might be questioned.

Document G

SUMMARIZE – Pasquier describes the impact in France of Napoleon's reports from Egypt.

ANALYZE – This document could help to legitimize Napoleon's claims to support the Muslims as stated in earlier documents.

CRITICIZE – Assuming that Pasquier wrote his memoirs after the fall of the empire, he might feel somewhat vindicated in his negative assessment of Napoleon.

Outside Evidence:

- Napoleon's rapid rise to power

- Napoleon's strategies for gaining power

Possible Categories of Evidence:

- Negative impact: A, D

- Positive impact: B, C, E, F

- Influence of French culture: C, E, F

- No attempt to impact: B, D, G, Napoleon's rise to power, Napoleon's strategies for gaining power

6. ITALIAN IMMIGRATION TO ARGENTINA

Exercise Question: Analyze the extent to which Italian immigration to Argentina in the late 19th and early 20th centuries was beneficial to both countries.

Document A

SUMMARIZE – Article 23 of Argentina's 1853 constitution states that the government will encourage unrestricted immigration of farmers, industrialists, and teachers from European countries.

ANALYZE – The document supports the notion that the Argentine government believed in 1853 that European immigrants would bring a benefit to Argentina.

CRITICIZE – Since this was a part of the national constitution, it can be assumed that at least those responsible for writing the constitution and those with the power to affect the constitution agreed that European immigration to Argentina would be beneficial. Additionally, since this clause remained in the constitution through at least two revisions until 1994, it appears as though European immigration to Argentina continued to be seen as a benefit to the country.

Document B

SUMMARIZE – The document suggests that Italians may be predisposed (by geography and economics) to emigration from Italy. It also claims that many of these emigrants have repeatedly returned to Italy and sent their American earnings back to their families who remained in Italy, and that these practices have been encouraged by the Italian government because of their benefits to the Italian economy. Additionally, it is noted that most of these migrants have gone to Argentina. The author ends with a cautionary note that the economic benefits of Italian emigration to the Americas may be ending due to new US immigration restrictions and the desire of some Italians to remain in America.

ANALYZE – This document provides reasons that Italian immigration to Argentina might have been valuable to the Italian economy. It also points to some outside forces that could limit the flow of immigrants.

CRITICIZE – This is a journal article from the late-19th century written by a US immigration official. It is difficult to identify any ulterior motives beyond simple analysis of the evidence; however, it can be assumed that the document will carry some American bias since the author is a US official.

Document C

SUMMARIZE – This chart shows the occupational distribution of immigrants to Argentina between 1857 and 1924. It appears from the statistics that, although agricultural workers continue to dominate the immigrant population, general laborers and professionals make up increasing percentages over time. Overall, professionals never account for more than 1-2% of the whole.

ANALYZE – This document might be used to support an argument that immigrants to Argentina have been generally low-skilled and, therefore, not so beneficial to advancing the Argentine economy – perhaps even taking jobs from native Argentinians. It might also be used to illustrate the extent to which immigration has, in fact, transformed the Argentine workforce.

CRITICIZE – The document was part of a research effort by a pioneer in demographic studies, and it is published in a professional journal that may not be widely distributed. It is unlikely that any attempt at

US propaganda would be distributed in such an obscure publication, so the evidence is likely authentic. That said, since this is a pioneering study, it is possible that the author's methods were somewhat rough and so may have yielded skewed results.

Document D

SUMMARIZE – The graph compares US and Argentine stock prices across 25 years (1906–1930). It shows that Argentine stock prices compared favorably to those of US stocks—even outperforming them in the first 8 years – until about 1921 when US stocks began to skyrocket.

ANALYZE – Since stock prices are often used as an indication of economic productivity, this document (in combination with Document C) could be used to support the argument that the Argentine economy was healthy and productive during the years of greatest immigration. Additionally, given what we know now about the US stock market in the 1920s, even the last few years of the graph seem to support Argentine economic stability.

CRITICIZE – The graph is taken from a report by the US Federal Reserve in 1997. By that date, it is likely that statisticians were working with reliable data.

Document E

SUMMARIZE – This graph compares Italian emigration to a variety of specific countries, including Argentina, between 1876 and 1940. According to the graph, Italian emigration to Argentina peaked in the 1880s, then gradually declined as emigration to the US increased until the 1910s when emigrants to the US fell off sharply and those heading to Argentina peaked again.

ANALYZE – This document serves to support the contention made in Document B that Italian immigration to the US would fall off in response to new US immigration restrictions. Additionally, along with Document C, this graph helps to explain the increase in Italian immigration to Argentina through the early decades of the 20th century.

CRITICIZE – Because this is another academic research report with presumably very little distribution, the author, an economics professor, has no obvious agenda except to study the data.

Document F

SUMMARIZE – This OAS report suggests reasons for European (especially Spanish and Italian) immigration to Argentina in the late-19th and early-20th centuries. It specifies the poor economic and volatile political situation in newly unified Italy as reasons for increased Italian emigration, as well as the lucrative opportunities for farmers and industrial workers in Argentina to help explain why Italians went there.

ANALYZE – This secondary source document provides authoritative support for several of the conclusions we drew from the earlier primary source documents. It can be used to support the argument that Italian emigration to Argentina benefitted the immigrants by providing more pay for the same work. If these immigrants to Argentina sent money home to Italy, as was suggested in Document B, then the benefits of working in Argentina were also transferred to the Italian economy.

CRITICIZE – Like so many of the other documents in this question, this one is a professional report. Without any additional information regarding the purpose of this report, we can assume its general authenticity and reliability.

Document G

SUMMARIZE – This chart shows GDP per capita statistics for Argentina and Italy between 1820 and 1990. According to these statistics, Italy produced nearly twice the output per capita as Argentina in 1820. Argentina's per capita production increased from that moment until it surpassed that of Italy in 1880. It continued to grow rapidly until it was nearly double the Italian level in 1920. From that point, Italian economic growth gained ground on the Argentine per capita GDP until it once again surpassed Argentina in the 1960s.

ANALYZE – While this document might be used to demonstrate the benefits to Argentina of Italian immigration, it could also be used to show that those benefits were not really shared with the Italian state. In the long run, of course, Italian growth may have shown gains, but, taken together with Document E, it seems that the benefits came when Italian immigration waned.

CRITICIZE – This chart is taken from a chapter of a 2014 book of essays on global well-being. Although it is certainly possible that this book is attempting to support some specific opinion about the well-being of the world's peoples, since we have no insight into that purpose, we can assume the evidence is reliable. Additionally, since this chapter is written by an economist, it is likely that her GDP per capita statistics are accurate.

Outside Evidence:

- Mussolini rose to power promising to revitalize a lagging economy

- Cavour (Italian PM, leader of unification, and proponent of industrialization) died in 1861

- Italy's poor natural resources and farmland could not support growing population in mid-1800s

Possible Categories of Evidence:

- Migration supported by government policies: A, B

- Migration motivated by economic situation: B, F, E, Italy poor in natural resources and farmland

- Argentina benefitted: C, D, E, G

- Italy benefitted: B, E, F

- Italy did not benefit: C, E, G, Mussolini's rise

- Emigration did not cause Italy's economic problems: B, poor natural resources and farmland, Cavour died

7. DECOLONIZATION

Exercise Question: Describe and analyze the various attitudes toward decolonization from 1930 to 1960.

Document A

SUMMARIZE – Gandhi criticizes British rule of India and promises to work for independence.

ANALYZE – The document can be used to support an argument about the view of decolonization from within the colony.

CRITICIZE – It would be difficult for a student who knows much about Gandhi to argue that this interview was in any way self-serving. However, Gandhi may have intended for his words to inspire other Indians to follow his example.

Document B

SUMMARIZE – The statement says that Burma is currently unfit for self-rule and must remain a colony until it can be made ready for independence.

ANALYZE – This document can be used as evidence of at least one reason for resistance against decolonization.

CRITICIZE – This British statement could be an attempt to hold onto the last strands of a dying empire. Why should the British give up this colony if they can convince the rest of the world that they are doing right by the Burmese people?

Document C

SUMMARIZE – Sukarno calls for unity in opposition to colonialism.

ANALYZE – The document is evidence of one view of colonialism and implies a view of decolonization.

CRITICIZE – Sukarno, president of the newly independent Indonesia, could be expected to oppose colonialism and to try to organize other African and Asian independent states to join this view.

Document D

SUMMARIZE – Nehru calls for the nations of Africa and Asia to avoid alignment with the communists or non-communists. He implies that alignment is akin to colonialism.

ANALYZE – The document can be evidence that former colonies oppose anything that even seems colonial.

CRITICIZE – As in Document C, Nehru's view is to be expected from the leader of a newly independent nation.

Document E

SUMMARIZE – The French government affirms its right to organize French colonies in any way it sees fit to improve the financial well-being of France and the colonies.

ANALYZE – The document is evidence of the French view of the legitimacy of colonial rule.

CRITICIZE – Having just lost Vietnam in 1954, France may be trying to avoid further imperial losses by affirming its "honorable" intentions within other French colonies.

Document F

SUMMARIZE – Sadat speaks out against colonialism and calls for opposition from all former colonies.

ANALYZE – The document is evidence of the views of the colonized.

CRITICIZE – Again, as president of a recently independent country, Sadat could be expected to oppose colonialism in any form.

Document G

SUMMARIZE – The UN states that colonialism should end immediately and that a lack of "readiness" is an inadequate argument to delay independence.

ANALYZE – The document shows a widespread view of colonialism.

CRITICIZE – Because France and Britain were both powerful members of the UN in 1960, the passage of this declaration is strong evidence of a shift in world opinion regarding colonialism.

Outside Evidence:

- Salt March

- Statute of Westminster (1931)

Possible Categories of Evidence:

- Support among colonists: A, C, D, F, Salt March

- Opposition outside colonies: B, E, Statute of Westminster

- Necessity: B, E, G

- Alignment is colonization: C, D

Step 3

Part A— Thesis Recognition

1. COLLAPSE OF CLASSICAL EMPIRES

Exercise Question: *Analyze the reasons for the decline and collapse of the classical empires in the period from 100 CE to 600 CE.*

A. (1+) This thesis addresses all tasks by clearly recognizing the time period, identifying relevant empires, and enumerating explicit reasons for their decline. This is a historically defensible position with analytical categories that can be explored further within the body of the essay.

B. (1) While this thesis identifies the task and pin-points relevant civilizations, the reasons for the collapse and decline are too generic. Although it earns credit, it barely establishes an acceptable line of reasoning.

C. (0) This thesis simply restates the question.

D. (0) While this thesis has recognized the period and identified collapsing empires, the thesis does not demonstrate an understanding of causation because the thesis does not include the causes of the collapse and decline.

E. (0) Another restatement of the question.

F. (0) While this thesis makes a strong argument "assessing" the notion that the empires fell, it fails to address the task set out in the question—"analyze." This student might know plenty of history but failed to answer the question!

G. (1) This thesis makes a strong argument analyzing the fall of the Han Empire, but fails to address the others. While it may earn the thesis point on the new rubric, the essay will likely fall short because of its narrow scope.

2. CONSEQUENCES OF EXPANDING TRADE

Exercise Question: Evaluate the effects of expanding trade routes from 600 CE to 1450 CE.

A. (0) While this thesis identifies the task and pinpoints relevant regions, the categories are too generic. Unlike choice B in #1 above, these categories have no modifier to help establish a line of reasoning.

B. (1+) This thesis addresses all tasks by clearly recognizing the time period, identifying relevant regions of the world, and enumerating explicit effects of trade. This is a historically defensible position with a clear line of reasoning that can be further explored within the body of the essay.

C. (0) This thesis simply restates the question.

D. (0) Another restatement of the question.

E. (0) While this thesis has recognized the period and identified relevant trade routes, the thesis does not demonstrate an understanding of the consequences because the thesis does not include the effects of increasing trade.

F. (1) This thesis statement provides a clear argument for the effects of the Indian Ocean Trade Route; however, its narrow focus on one region in this period makes it unlikely to support a strong essay.

G. (0) While the thesis states a clear position and a historically defensible line of reasoning, it fails to address the prompt directly—it argues for causes rather than effects.

3. SHIFTS IN EURASIAN INFLUENCES

Exercise Question: Analyze the extent to which the source of influence in Eurasia shifted between 1450 and 1600.

A. (0) Although this thesis addresses the prompt, it fails to establish a line of reasoning.

B. (1) The thesis states an argument addressing the prompt and establishes a line of reasoning. Although it will likely earn the Thesis point on the rubric, it neglects to specify the time frame of the argument and might lead to a discussion that is outside the scope of this question.

C. (0) This thesis might earn the point for stating a clear position ("stayed in the West") with a minimal line of reasoning ("The Renaissance"), but you should strive to do much better than this.

D. (1+) This thesis states a position and establishes a clear line of reasoning. Furthermore, the categories of evidence used in the thesis set up a great argument.

E. (0) Simply restates the question.

F. (0) Fails to establish a line of reasoning.

G. (1) This thesis states a position and a line of reasoning but might lead to "half" of an argument in the essay. It implies that Chinese influence waned, but fails to suggest who's influence increased in its place.

4. INDUSTRIALIZATION AND SOCIAL CHANGE

Exercise Question: Analyze the impact of the Industrial Revolution on the lower classes of Europe in the 19th century.

A. (1+) Somewhat awkward at the start, this thesis is clear, logical, and analytical.

B. (1) Overstated! Although overstatement is generally ill-advised on the AP test, with the right evidence and good analysis, this thesis could lend itself to a very nice essay.

C. (0) The structure of this thesis is okay, but the evidence mentioned seems to imply that the author will be writing about the American Industrial Revolution, in which case it will be off-topic.

D. (1) This is a good, concise thesis, and with further analysis in the rest of the opening paragraph, it could yield a top-scoring essay.

E. (1) Although this goes further than restating the question because it states that the lower classes were disadvantaged, the author may have to work very hard to force these generic categories onto this question.

F. (1) This thesis addresses the tasks and terms, but it is very general because it lacks any hint of categories of evidence. It may be, however, a better start than choice E because it does not have to adhere to any contrived categories.

G. (1) This is a very nice thesis. If the author addresses the WHYs of these categories somewhere in the opening paragraph, it could be a good foundation for a top essay.

5. ITALIAN IMMIGRATION TO ARGENTINA

Exercise Question: *Analyze the extent to which Italian immigration to Argentina in the late 19th and early 20th centuries was beneficial to both countries.*

A. (0) This is a simple restatement of the question.

B. (0) Although this thesis hints at a basic line of reasoning, it is unlikely to earn the point. You can do much better!

C. (0) "…socially, politically, and economically" does not constitute an acceptable line of reasoning. This is no better than choice A.

D. (1) Addresses the tasks and terms directly with a clearly stated position and establishes a historically defensible line of reasoning.

E. (1+) This is the more analytical version of choice D. In addition to a clear position and line of reasoning, this thesis begins to allude to the "HOWs" of its categories of evidence.

F. (1+) Although this thesis states a position counter to the one in choice E, it is equally strong and analytical.

G. (0) This thesis sounds just as strong as those in choices E and F, however, this one fails to answer the assigned question.

H. (1) This thesis states a position and establishes a line of reasoning. It's not great, but it does earn credit.

6. MUSLIM LEAGUE VS. QUEBECOIS SEPARATISTS

Exercise Question: In what ways do the Muslim League Movement of British India in the early 1900s and the Quebecois Separatist Movement of Canada from the 1960s share similar motivations?

A. (1+) This thesis addresses all tasks and terms of the question with three somewhat analytical categories of evidence.

B. (0) Although this thesis resembles choice A in format, it actually discusses "goals" rather than "motivations." It addresses the task but not the terms.

C. (0) This statement addresses the task but with insufficiently specific categories of evidence.

D. (1) This thesis mentions secession as a goal of both, thus addressing the question briefly, but it focuses on the contrasting motivations of both groups. It addresses the task and terms minimally, but is likely to lead to an argument that is partially off-task.

E. (0) This thesis states a position that may not be historically defensible and fails to establish a valid line of reasoning.

F. (0) Although this sentence is stated more correctly than choice E, its position is also historically indefensible.

G. (0) This thesis looks like it has established a line of reasoning, but without further explanation of "politically," "economically," and "socially," it will not earn credit.

Part B—Analytical Thesis Development

1. THE NEOLITHIC REVOLUTION

Exercise Question: *Analyze the extent to which the Neolithic Revolution served as a cause for the establishment of civilizations.*

Tasks: "Analyze"

Terms: "Neolithic Revolution" "cause" "civilizations"

Question Restated: In what ways was the Neolithic Revolution a cause of civilization and in what ways was it not?

Sample Thesis: Although the basic social organization of the earliest agricultural civilizations had been well-established by their nomadic ancestors, the technologies of the Neolithic Revolution, specifically in agriculture, allowed for the accumulation of surplus food and supplies which provided formerly nomadic peoples with incentives to establish larger sedentary settlements that necessitated formalized governments, specialized labor, and trade.

2. HORTICULTURE TO AGRICULTURE

Exercise Question: *Analyze the extent to which agriculture and pastoralism caused transformations in human societies.*

Task: "Analyze"

Terms: "agriculture" "pastoralism" "transformations" "human societies"

Question Restated: In what ways did agriculture and pastoralism cause changes in human societies and in what ways did they not?

Sample Thesis: To the extent that women had managed the food gathering and horticultural responsibilities, gender roles were transformed with the introduction of animal labor and agriculture; however, to the extent that the basic group organization and religious beliefs predated the agricultural revolution, most aspects of human societies changed little with agriculture and pastoralism.

3. UNIVERSAL RELIGIONS IN THE CLASSICAL PERIOD

Exercise Question: Analyze the reasons for the rapid expansion of universal religions across Eurasia in the classical period (600 BCE - 600 CE).

Task: "Analyze"

Terms: "reasons" "rapid expansion" "universal religions" "Eurasia" "classical period"

Question Restated: Why did universal religions spread across Eurasia (600 BCE – 600 CE)?

Sample Thesis: In the classical period, universal religions (Christianity and Buddhism) expanded rapidly across Eurasia because they established missionary groups to spread their messages, produced written texts to codify their beliefs, and validated existing political systems to more easily win converts.

4. GROWTH OF TRADING CITIES

Exercise Question: Compare and contrast the reasons for the growth of trading cities in different parts of the world from 600 CE to 1450 CE.

Task: "Compare and Contrast"

Terms: "reasons for" "growth" "trading cities" "600 CE to 1450 CE"

Question Restated: What are similar and different reasons for the growth of urban areas in Europe, Asia, Africa, and America?

Sample Thesis: In the period from 600 to 1450, trading cities grew across Afro-Eurasia because of pre-existing trade routes and improvements in technology, however, differences in local governance influenced the structure and function of many commercial hubs.

5. ISLAMIC KINGDOMS

Exercise Question: *Compare and contrast the key characteristics of the two primary Islamic kingdoms of the 16th century, the Ottomans and the Safavids.*

Tasks: "Compare," "contrast"

Terms: "key characteristics," "primary Islamic kingdoms," "16th century," "Ottomans," "Safavids"

Question Restated: In what ways were the 16th century Ottoman and Safavid empires alike, and in which ways were they different.

Sample Thesis: Although the sixteenth-century Ottoman and Safavid empires had similar origins, the two primary Islamic kingdoms were culturally disparate and these differences led to unique governing styles.

6. INDUSTRIALIZATION OF JAPAN AND BRITAIN

Exercise Question: *Compare and contrast the process of industrialization in Japan with the earlier industrialization of Britain.*

Tasks: "Compare," "contrast"

Terms: "process" "industrialization" "Japan" "Britain"

Question Restated: In what ways were the processes of industrialization in Japan and Britain alike, and in what ways were they different?

Sample Thesis: Although Japan and Britain approached industrialization from similar perspectives as island nations with independent spirits and strong navies, the process of industrialization itself differed significantly between the two states – Britain was slow and haphazard while Japan was quick and well-planned.

7. INTERWAR ART

Exercise Question: *To what extent was Interwar Art unique from art of the period immediately before World War I?*

Tasks: "To what extent"

Terms: "art," "interwar," "reaction to WWI"

Question Restated: In what ways did art react to WWI between 1918 and 1939? In what ways did art NOT react to WWI between 1918 and 1939?

Sample Thesis: To the extent that Irrationalism in literature and the visual arts grew out of the disillusionment in the rational ideas that allowed for such massive destruction, interwar art was driven by reaction to World War I; to the extent, however, that many Lost Generation writers and painters used prewar techniques to make political statements, interwar art was more evolution than revolution.

8. WWII CONFERENCES AND COLD WAR POLICY

Exercise Question: *Analyze the impact of WWII Allied conferences on subsequent Cold War policy.*

Tasks: "Analyze"

Terms: "impact of WWII allied conferences," "cold war policy"

Question Restated: In what ways or for what reasons was cold war policy affected by WWII allied conferences?

Sample Thesis: The exclusion of the Soviets from the earliest Allied conferences, animosity between Stalin and Churchill, and an American diplomacy that avoided direct confrontation among the Allies fueled an East-West distrust that would become a hallmark of cold war policy.

Step 4

Presenting the Argument

1. COLLAPSE OF CLASSICAL EMPIRES

Exercise Question: *Analyze the reasons for the decline and collapse of the classical empires in the period from 100 CE to 600 CE.*

Sample Opening Paragraph: The early part of the first millennium of the Common Era saw the emergence of several groups of nomadic warriors from there steppe homelands, often driven by the same population growth that propelled the expansion of more sedentary kingdoms. As the two groups clashed on the frontiers, the military prowess of the mounted nomads became immediately apparent and exerted a new strain on already decaying empires. Furthermore, with the emergence and acceptance of belief systems like Christianity and Daoism, the political system and traditional culture became challenged by an internal struggle. Classical empires like the Han, Gupta, and Roman collapsed by 600 CE because of the constant threat of foreign invaders, the emergence of religious beliefs counter to traditional culture, and the mismanagement of the political administration of the empire.

2. CONSEQUENCES OF EXPANDING TRADE

Exercise Question: *Evaluate the effects of expanding trade routes from 600 CE to 1450 CE.*

Sample Opening Paragraph: As classical empires collapsed and new, more cosmopolitan, empires emerged in their places, "global" exchange networks expanded across Afro-Eurasia and would eventually cross the Atlantic to the Americas. With the expanding diffusion of goods and ideas along new and established trade routes, a new concept of "the world" emerged. Boundaries of the old isolated world zones were gradually disintegrating, giving way to globalized languages and universal religions. The expansion of trade networks in Africa, Asia, and the Americas from 600 to 1450 created a diffusion of languages like Arabic, an exchange of religious practices like Buddhism, and a sharing of technologies like ironworks.

3. SHIFTS IN EURASIAN INFLUENCES

Exercise Question: Analyze the extent to which the source of influence in Eurasia shifted between 1450 and 1600.

Sample Opening Paragraph: As late as the early 15th century, China remained the dominant cultural power in Eurasia. The culture of the Tang and Song dynasties had spread west for centuries via the Silk Road, and Mongol dominance under the Yuan Dynasty expanded China's exchange networks even further. The Ming Dynasty used overseas expeditions to affirm Chinese supremacy and bring Chinese goods and ideas directly to India, Africa, and the Eastern Mediterranean. By 1450, however, the new Ming emperor decided to end Chinese maritime trade, ceding its dominance of the seas. The simultaneous cessation of Chinese sea trade, a surge in Portuguese and Spanish navigation, and the intellectual Renaissance in Italy helped to shift Eurasian influence to the west between 1450 and 1600.

4. INDUSTRIALIZATION AND SOCIAL CHANGE

Exercise Question: Analyze the impact of the Industrial Revolution on the lower classes of Europe in the 19th century.

Sample Opening Paragraph: Industrialization was responsible for revolutionary changes across Europe. From manufacturing to transportation, industrialization transformed many European cities within a generation—but not everyone shared in the good fortune. As a result of the Industrial Revolution, lower-class families were broken down because all members of the family needed to work outside the home; lower- class children were less educated because their families needed them to work from a very young age; and lower-class women were often driven to prostitution because it paid more than factory work. While farmers were able to maintain traditional family dynamics, many of the urban poor were forced to abandon traditional lifestyles for the sake of economic survival. Because every member of the family was often forced to work long hours outside the home, lower- class children remained uneducated and young girls, sometimes alone and uneducated in the city, resorted to prostitution to make ends meet.

5. ITALIAN IMMIGRATION TO ARGENTINA

Exercise Question: *Analyze the extent to which Italian immigration to Argentina in the late 19th and early 20th centuries was beneficial to both countries.*

Sample Opening Paragraph: The 19th century saw nationalist movements around the world, including those that led to Italian unification and Argentine independence. In general, these movements, even when they resulted in increased autonomy, often failed to bring immediate economic relief to the masses. Political and economic instability created uncertain futures, so many of the recently-established states were forced to experiment with new ideas for survival. The policies of Argentina and Italy combined to create one of the greatest migrations of the era. While Argentina may have reaped the greatest benefits from Italian immigration in the 19th and 20th centuries in the form of much-needed agricultural and industrial labor as well as professional expertise, it is also true that Italy's troubled economy benefited from the earnings sent home to support the immigrants' families.

6. MUSLIM LEAGUE VS. QUEBECOIS SEPARATISTS

Exercise Question: In what ways do the Muslim League
Movement of British India in the early 1900s and the
Quebecois Separatist Movement of Canada from the 1960s
share similar motivations?

Sample Opening Paragraph: India, like Canada, was a British
colony before gaining its independence. Unlike Canada, however,
India remained a colony well into the 20th century. As the
Second World War ended, and after years of peaceful protests
led by Gandhi, India gained its autonomy. The population of
India was religiously divided, primarily between Hindus and
Muslims, and Muslim leaders had formed the Muslim League
to protect the rights of Muslims within the majority Hindu India.
Eventually, their concerns led the Muslim league to push for
an independent Muslim state. Meanwhile in Canada, almost a
century after its independence, the French-speaking population
of Quebec, blaming the English-speaking Canadians for their
economic troubles, began to organize their own separatist
movement. Although both groups felt their minority status was
the root of their troubles, and both movements can be described
as "nationalist" at times, the Muslim League was primarily
concerned about political freedom, whereas the Quebecois were
mostly worried about economics.

Part A—Analyzing Evidence for the LEQ

1. THE EARLIEST URBAN SOCIETIES

Exercise Question: *Evaluate the extent to which the earliest urban societies, 5,000 years ago, laid the foundations for the development of complex civilizations.*

Sample Thesis: Although the earliest urban societies adopted governing structures and economic diversification that would be parts of later more complex civilizations, because of the increased complexity necessary to deal with rapid population growth, later social structures became much more than simply larger versions of their predecessors.

Sample Body Paragraph: From the earliest river civilizations, the accumulation of large numbers of anonymous people in urban centers created a necessity for more formal governing structures. Even the small urban centers needed administrators and diplomats. As cities grew so did the surplus of food, and more people engaged in non-farming activities, forming several social classes based on the jobs they performed. New government officials found it useful to create rules controlling the interactions of these social groups. Eventually, the rules became formalized laws, such as the Babylonian Code of Hammurabi. Just as Hammurabi's Code was adapted from earlier law codes of Ur, it became the model for Roman Laws of the later millennia.

2. TRADE NETWORKS OF AFRO-EURASIA

Exercise Question: *Analyze the changes and continuities produced by trade networks throughout Afro-Eurasia from 800 BCE to 900 CE.*

Sample Thesis: While the various regions of Afro-Eurasia remained separate and independent through most of the time period, extensive trade routes that crisscrossed these continents led to an exchange of goods and ideas that advanced and elevated all involved.

Sample Body Paragraph: One of the greatest advancements in European warfare was the cavalry, but this achievement would have been completely impossible without the introduction of the stirrup from Asia. During Europe's classical period, ancient Greeks and Romans relied primarily on the infantry to fight wars. After Central Asian invaders swept across Europe, however, Europeans began to adopt the stirrup in battle. A second example of technology that traveled along the Indian Ocean and then the Mediterranean was the lateen sail. This maritime innovation allowed ships to sail into the wind, increasing the speed and reliability in both trade and warfare. In both examples, extensive trade networks stretching across Afro-Eurasia led to the spread of technology that advanced civilization.

3. CODIFICATION OF RELIGIOUS TRADITIONS

Exercise Question: *To what extent did the codification of religious traditions prior to the first millennium CE mark a turning point in world history?*

Sample Thesis: The codification of religious traditions marked a turning point as civilizations adopted them into their legal and social systems, however, the persistence of uncodified beliefs like shamanism demonstrates a distinct continuity in the same time period.

Sample Body Paragraph: Judaism and Confucianism provided clear guidelines for the behavior of their followers allowing their beliefs to be codified by emerging states at the turn of the first millennium. For Judaism, the Ten Commandments clearly defined the right and wrong actions of its followers. Therefore, as Jews moved throughout the Middle East and Europe, these ideas of "thou shall not kill" became adopted by institutions in Babylon and Rome. In China, Confucianism addressed the importance of relationships and maintaining respect for authority. The government passed laws in the interest of the people and the dynasty maintained its power. Confucius noted, "Let the ruler be the ruler". For both Judaism and Confucianism, their ethics became the legal tradition of the early empires in the classical period.

4. CONTINUITY AND CHANGE IN DYNASTIC CHINA

Exercise Question: Describe and explain significant continuities and changes in the Chinese political system from the Tang Dynasty to the Mongol empire.

Sample Thesis: Although the political system changed from native rule under the Tang and Song to Mongol rule in the Yuan Dynasty, the Chinese government retained its reliance on the scholar class and Confucian ethics.

Sample Body Paragraph: In the centuries of Tang and Song rule, Chinese emperors maintained a centralized government using the civil service system and strict adherence to Confucian ethics to elevate Han elites to powerful administrative positions. Genghis Khan and the Mongols descended on the Western Xia in the early 13th century, and when his grandson, Kublai Khan finally completed the conquest of the Southern Song, he gutted the palace of its Han administrators and filled those positions with his Mongol brethren. The new Yuan emperor eliminated the Civil Service System that had given so much advantage to the Han Chinese, and instead appointed his most trusted associates to administer the state.

5. IMPACT OF TECHNOLOGY, 1900–1918

Exercise Question: Identify and assess the impact of new technology on the conduct of the Great War.

Sample Thesis: New technology helped to spur on the militarism that preceded the Great War, and new weapons shifted the military advantage to the defense and ultimately created the means by which over 30 million men would be lost in the war.

Sample Body Paragraph: Although the militarism of the early-20th century was motivated, at least in part, by the nationalism of the time period, it was certainly accelerated by new technology. Advances in steel manufacture allowed for improvements in naval vessels, armored vehicles, and artillery weapons. The Anglo-German race to build bigger and better navies, symbolized by the dreadnought, exemplifies the impact of steel technology on the war effort. In fact, it was this naval race that led Germany to explore submarine technology and create a weapon that would ultimately draw the United States into the Great War. In addition to naval developments, new technology improved land warfare through newer and better guns, including larger rifled artillery weapons and machine guns, the latter of which was perhaps most responsible for shifting the advantage to the defensive army.

6. RAPID ADVANCES IN SCIENCE IN THE 20TH CENTURY

Exercise Question: Evaluate the extent to which rapid advances in science in the 20th century altered our understanding of the universe and the natural world, and led to the development of new technologies.

Sample Thesis: Scientific discovery in the computer age accelerated our understanding of the universe and the natural world exponentially through advanced speed of calculation which allowed for future modeling of current trends, expanded connectivity among researchers permitting much more rapid exchange of ideas, and, as a result of these expanded networks of exchange, ever more rapid innovation and new technology.

Sample Body Paragraph: While the scientific community has had a history of open communication allowing researchers to build on the work of their peers around the world, this interaction went on primarily in printed journals and annual professional society meetings. With the advent of internet connectivity, it became possible for scientists to communicate their findings immediately, speeding innovation and invention. A typical example was the Human Genome Project. Conducted online by geneticists from around the world, researchers were able to map human DNA in just 13 years. Without the computer, this work would have been impossible.

Part B—Analyzing Evidence for the DBQ

1. DAOISM AND CONFUCIANISM

Exercise Question: *Compare and contrast the cultural and political effects of Daoism and Confucianism on China.*

Sample Thesis: Daoism and Confucianism had a significant effect on Chinese culture as both aided the development of a uniform written language but had varying effects on Chinese politics and society as they placed different values on the importance of education and political authority.

Sample Body Paragraph: Daoism and Confucianism differed strongly on their views on education having different impacts on Chinese culture and education. While Laozi's Tao Te Ching (Document E) and the Confucian inscription (Document F) both demonstrated the importance in sharing information via a written language, the core beliefs of the faith disagreed on the value of education. For Laozi, the best doing is "nondoing" and his student, Zhuangzi, supported that view when he encouraged his followers to avoid education (Document B). For Confucius, however, education was essential to social order. While Zilu's 19th century sketch is not from the period nor from China, it does demonstrate the importance of education on Confucian followers in the classical period (Document G). Zilu, a Confucian disciple, spends day and night learning demonstrating the impact on education and the acquisition of knowledge on Chinese culture. Thus, Confucianism and Daoism had conflicting effects on the education of Chinese people as one sought to encourage academic pursuits and the other desired to limit its impact on everyday life.

2. MARGINALIZED PEOPLES

Exercise Question: *Analyze the influence of patriarchy and hierarchy on the treatment of marginalized people from 600 CE to 1450 CE.*

Sample Thesis: From 600 CE to 1450 CE, marginalized people, like unfree labor and women as well as ethnic groups different from the ruling government, were often times mistreated by the existing patriarchy and hierarchy.

Sample Body Paragraph: Throughout Europe and South America, unfree labor in the form of serfdom was employed by the hierarchical government to ensure economic success. In the case of European manorialism, the peasants worked the land belonging to their lord. In the *Book of Hours* (Document F), the Duke of Berry commissions an illustration of life on his manor. Since it was a commissioned work, the artists construct the image based on the Duke's specifications. The Duke of Berry desired to show his power by portraying his serfs hard at work even in the winter months. The peasants plow the fields and cut wood while living in a one room hut. The same treatment of unfree labor is seen in the Inca Empire because both regions needed to tie labor to land in order to ensure agricultural production. The Incan Empire relied on the Mit'a System (Document G). With government work projects, these Incan laborers worked the land and planted the crops. On both continents, unfree laborers were marginalized by the existing hierarchical system.

3. THE CONCEPT OF LOVE

Exercise Question: *Compare and contrast the concept of "love" across Eurasia and the ways in which it impacted gender relations from 400 to 1300 CE.*

Sample Thesis: Although "love" and gender relations differed in their details across Eurasia, the complete submission of the woman and the general entitlement of the man were common features.

Sample Body Paragraph: No matter the specific details of love and gender roles, submission of the women was expected everywhere across Eurasia. An Indian play describes a scene in which a king startles three young women and expresses his desire for one of them. At the king's command, two of the friends exit the scene, leaving the third to submit to the will of the king (Document A). Another example comes from the *Tale of Genji* in Japan. In the excerpt, a young girl is essentially raped by a drunk king (Document D). Both of these examples are from popular literature of the time period, implying that this sort of behavior is not only acceptable but expected.

4   ITALIAN IMMIGRATION TO ARGENTINA

Exercise Question: *Analyze the extent to which Italian immigration to Argentina in the late 19th and early 20th centuries was beneficial to both countries.*

Sample Thesis: While Argentina may have reaped the greatest benefits from Italian immigration in the 19th and 20th centuries in the form of much-needed agricultural and industrial labor as well as professional expertise, it is also true that Italy's troubled economy benefited from the earnings sent home to support the immigrants' families.

Sample Body Paragraph: The benefits of Italian immigration to the new Argentine Republic were extensive and openly recognized by Argentina, however, the newly-unified Kingdom of Italy also benefited from the migrations. In the late 19th and early 20th centuries, many of the Italian immigrants worked in Argentina and sent money home to their families back in Italy. For years, these same "birds of passage" returned to their homes again and again (Document B). The immediate impact was evident as several parts of Italy outpaced their neighbors in economic progress during the period. Long term effects may be supported by the eventual increased growth rate in Italy in the mid-20th century (Document G). Since the data in this document was gathered for no obvious reason beyond academic study, it seems reasonable to believe that it is a reliable source of evidence.

5 DENG XIAOPING IN CHINA'S ECONOMIC LIBERALIZATION

Exercise Question: *Analyze the role of Deng Xiaoping in China's economic liberalization beginning in the late 1970s.*

Sample Thesis: Deng Xiaoping actively pushed the liberalization of the Chinese economy through promoting foreign investment, encouraging ground-level changes, and connecting liberalism to Communist ideals and traditional Chinese values.

Sample Body Paragraph: Deng Xiaoping used Communist ideals to inspire more competitive practices within the Communist model. According to Tisdell, Deng used the ideal of "each according to his work" to move away from the "iron bowl" syndrome responsible for the weak economic performance of the 1960s and 70s (Document A). This focus on individual performance and individual reward was even included in the official report of the Third Plenary Session (Document G). From that moment forward, Chinese farmers were encouraged to sell a share of their produce once they had satisfied the basic demands of the state. An industrious farmer could now improve his personal economic status by working harder than his neighbors. The overall effect on the Chinese economy was a sharp upturn in GDP, eventually creating one of the world's strongest economies and a "major global exporter" (Document F).

Step 5

Part C— Analytical Transitions

1. IMPACT ON ENVIRONMENT OF HUNTER-FORAGERS AND SETTLED SOCIETIES

Exercise Question: *Contrast how hunter-foragers and settled societies affected the environment.*

Sample Thesis: Hunter-Foragers and settled societies both relied on the natural environment for a food source but varied sharply as the size of the population impacted the structures erected and defenses built.

Sample Transition: The difference in size of the hunter-foragers and settled societies caused a dramatic difference in the structures built as hunter-foragers relied on temporary as well as movable housing instead urban, permanent settlements.

2. EXPANSION OF ISLAM

Exercise Question: *Assess the extent to which the promotion of Islam changed trade, warfare, and culture from 700 CE to 1453 CE.*

Sample Thesis: From 700 CE to 1453 CE, the expansion and promotion of Islam across the Middle East, North Africa and Europe caused small scale regional war as well as the crusades, improved existing trade routes like the Silk Road, and restored the mathematical, scientific, and intellectual pursuits.

Sample Transition: As Islam expanded, the language of Arabic emerged as the language of trade having a positive impact on pre-existing trade routes like the West Africa Trade Route and Silk Road.

3. THE COLUMBIAN EXCHANGE

Exercise Question: *To what extent was the Columbian Exchange mutually beneficial to Native Americans and Europeans?*

Sample Thesis: To the extent that plants and animals were exchanged to the benefit of both worlds, the Columbian Exchange was mutually beneficial; however, because the Native Americans were forced to abandon their beliefs for Christianity and afflicted with several European diseases, the Europeans gained a greater advantage from the exchange.

Sample Transition: Despite the long-term benefits to both hemispheres, the immediate impact of the Columbian Exchange held harsh repercussions for the Native Americans.

4. ITALIAN IMMIGRATION TO ARGENTINA

Exercise Question: *Analyze the extent to which Italian immigration to Argentina in the late 19th and early 20th centuries was beneficial to both countries.*

Sample Thesis: While Argentina may have reaped the greatest benefits from Italian immigration in the 19th and 20th centuries in the form of much-needed agricultural and industrial labor as well as professional expertise, it is also true that Italy's troubled economy benefited from the earnings sent home to support the immigrants' families.

Sample Transition: In addition to a massive force of unskilled labor that helped to build the necessary infrastructure at Buenos Aires, some Italian immigrants also brought needed professional skills to Argentina in the late-19th and early-20th centuries.

5. THE BOER WAR

Exercise Question: Analyze the ways in which the Boer War was portrayed in published works.

Sample Thesis: Published works of the early-20th century portrayed the British army in the Boer Wars as patriotic and courageous, but the same sources often criticized the war effort as ill guided and unnecessary.

Sample Transition: Many of the same sources that praised the British soldier for his courage criticized the war effort for its wrong-headedness.

6. GLOBALIZATION EFFECTS ON WORLD SOCCER

Exercise Question: Compare and contrast the effects of globalization on professional soccer clubs and World Cup national teams.

Sample Thesis: While the labor mobility of globalization has contributed to brain drain (or "leg drain") in professional soccer clubs, creating a few elite teams within each league, open borders and global marketing have helped World Cup soccer to rise to the top of all spectator sports worldwide.

Sample Transition: Despite the leg drain produced by player movement away from their home clubs to play for the richest teams internationally, the concentration of talent within these few elite teams has tended to elevate the level of play overall.

7. IMPACT OF EUROPEAN DOMINANCE IN THE EARLY 20TH C.

Exercise Question: *Evaluate the extent to which European dominance of the world at the beginning of the 20th century impacted the Middle East.*

Sample Thesis: Although European impact on the Middle East in the early 20th century included direct control of colonies in the region, and the eventual redrawing of borders as those colonies were granted independence, the greatest cultural influence came from the predominance of Islam in the region.

Sample Transition: Although the politics of the Middle East were definitely impacted by the actions of imperialist European nations, the culture of the region was dominated by the beliefs of Islam.

Step 6

Effective Closing Paragraphs

1. DEVELOPMENT OF THE RIVER VALLEY CIVILIZATIONS

Exercise Question: *Evaluate the extent to which there were similarities in the development of civilizations in the River Valleys.*

Sample Thesis: Early river valley civilizations were all based on an agricultural economy and institutions that developed around the flooding of their rivers, however, the details of those institutions differed according to the specific nature of their particular rivers.

Sample Closing Paragraph: Mesopotamia, the Nile, the Indus, and the Yellow River valleys all fostered the earliest sedentary civilizations, and each of these grew and prospered around its river-based farming economy. In addition to agricultural economies, all these early river civilizations also developed governments, religions, and social structures connected with the natural flood patterns of their rivers. When a river flooded regularly and predictably, like the Nile, the political, religious, and social institutions of that civilization exhibited stability and predictability. When, however, the rivers were violent and unpredictable, like the Tigris and Euphrates, they inspired more unstable civil institutions. Although all the early river civilizations shared an agricultural economy and civil structures linked to their river valleys, each river system exhibited its own unique flood pattern, so the details of each civilization's political, religious, and social institutions differed.

2. AGE OF EMPIRE IN THE CLASSICAL PERIOD

Exercise Question: *To what extent should the political unity from 600 BCE to 600 CE in world history be regarded as an "Age of Empire"?*

Sample Thesis: The label, "Age of Empire," may be justified by the imperial administrations of the Han Dynasty and the military expansion of the Roman and Persian empires, however, the rise of city-states in the Mayan kingdom undermines this periodization.

Sample Closing Paragraph: From the expansion of Persia and Rome to the construction of the imperial administrations, Eurasia saw the emergence of powerful empires while Mesoamerica continued to rely on city states to administrator laws and justice. In the Roman and Persian empires, the military was used in order to expand their borders and colonize neighboring people. With this expansion of borders, the governments in the Han and Roman empires began creating elaborate administrations to handle tax collection and maintenance of roads. While Eurasia embraced empire building in this era, Mesoamerican continued to rely on smaller city states as seen with Mayan civilization. A vast number of city states existed within the civilization allowing for the diffusion of goods and ideas without large amounts of conquest and centralized political oversight. The label, "Age of Empire," may be justified by the imperial administrations of the Han Dynasty and the military expansion of the Roman and Persian empires, however, the rise of city-states in the Mayan kingdom undermines this periodization.

3. CENTRALIZATION IN THE INTER-REGIONAL PERIOD

Exercise Question: *To what extent does the "Era of Centralization" accurately describe the global political systems from 600 CE to 1450 CE?*

Sample Thesis: The "Era of Centralization" accurately describes the dynasties of China and emerging Islamic states from 600 CE to 1450 CE, but does not describe the feudal system within Europe during that same time.

Sample Closing Paragraph: From 600 CE to 1450 CE, the "Era of Centralization" highly accurately describes the dynasties of China and emerging Islamic states, but does not describe the feudal system within Europe. In the Tang Dynasty, the emperors valued the growth of bureaucracy, the creation of a capital city, and the building of public works projects demonstrating the centralization of the state. In the Middle East, the Umayyad and Abbasid Empires began the process of centralization by establishing dynastic succession and founding Baghdad as a focal point. In addition, Arabic became the unifying language of the empires because Islam replaced local tribal languages. Nevertheless, "the Era of Centralization" does not accurately describe the political system in Europe, as small feudal kingdoms persisted without political urban centers, a unifying language, or a clear code of law. The "Era of Centralization" accurately describes the dynasties of China and emerging Islamic states from 600 CE to 1450 CE, but does not describe the feudal system within Europe during that same time.

4. THE AGE OF REVOLUTIONS

Exercise Question: In what ways was the Taiping Rebellion in China similar to the Independence Revolutions in Latin America?

Sample Thesis: Despite the fact that, unlike the Revolutions of Latin America, the Taiping Revolt faced no outside oppression, it was similar to the Independence Revolutions in that it sought to improve living standards for the local peasants by throwing off the yoke of oppression, and it was guided by a charismatic leader with humble origins.

Sample Closing Paragraph: In the Taiping rebellion, Chinese peasants fought unsuccessfully to overthrow the Qing rulers. The Qing were not foreign imperialists, but, for the peasant majority, their government exhibited the same oppressive characteristics as those seen in contemporary Latin American colonies –

resource depletion, political domination, and restrictive social classes. Despite the fact that, unlike the Revolutions of Latin America, the Taiping Revolt faced no outside oppression, it was similar to the Independence Revolutions in that it sought to improve living standards for the local peasants by throwing off the yoke of oppression, and it was guided by a charismatic leader with humble origins.

5. THE IMPACT OF TWENTIETH-CENTURY WARS

Exercise Question: *Analyze the impact of twentieth-century wars on TWO of the following regions: Africa, Asia, Oceania, and South America.*

Sample Thesis: Wars of the 20th century impacted Asia and Africa because the imperialist powers that engaged in those wars subordinated the local peoples in order to extract the natural resources of their lands, many of those lands also became the site of destructive battles, and eventually, when the fighting ended and the imperialists withdrew, the native peoples were left to rebuild with no support from their former oppressors.

Sample Closing Paragraph: The peoples of Asia and Africa were forced to endure some of the worst effects of the various wars of the twentieth century. The Middle East and northern Africa suffered through both World Wars, Vietnam and Korea were sites of imperialist invasions, and Sub-Saharan Africa supplied industrial resources for its imperial oppressors. The lands of both continents were devastated by conflict and depleted of their natural abundance. As each war ended and the aggressors retreated, the local peoples were left alone to pick up the pieces and rebuild. Wars of the 20th century impacted Asia and Africa because the imperialist powers that engaged in those wars subordinated the local peoples in order to extract the natural resources of their lands, many of those lands also became the site of destructive battles, and eventually, when the fighting ended and the imperialists withdrew, the native peoples were left to rebuild with no support from their former oppressors.

6. ENVIRONMENTAL CHALLENGES OF THE 21ST CENTURY

Exercise Question: *Analyze the ways in which economic policy interacts with environmental policy in the 21st century.*

Sample Thesis: While 21st century nations must find a balance between the cost of environmental policies that address global warming and the immediate and potential benefits of such policies, international leaders of government and business have recognized that inaction regarding the environment may be even more costly than action.

Sample Closing Paragraph: The Canadian Prime Minister outlined the concerns of many industrialized nations at the UN Climate Summit when he said that the "core principle" must be "balance." While most of the representatives at this 2007 meeting expressed concerns for the environment, several echoed Canada's temperance. In terms of the benefits of new environmental policies aimed at diminishing greenhouse gases, delegates included future economic positioning and survival of the planet, but the UN Secretary-General expressed an underlying fear that "the cost of inaction will far outweigh the cost of action." Nations overwhelmingly saw a need to find a balance between environmental and economic policy decisions, while remembering that inaction holds its own cost. While 21st century nations must find a balance between the cost of environmental policies that address global warming and the immediate and potential benefits of such policies, international leaders of government and business have recognized that inaction regarding the environment may be even more costly than action.

The Other Question Types

Multiple-Choice Questions

Document analysis for Questions 1–3.

SUMMARIZE – Socrates in his defense at his trial argues against the glorification of Athenian democracy. Instead of praising Athens for its justice and political systems, he criticizes the citizens of Athens for their lack of free speech and their political pettiness.

ANALYZE – This speech counters the traditional interpretation of Athens as the birthplace of democracy and free speech. While sources like Pericles Oration Speech recognize the positives of Athenian democracy, Socrates counters oftentimes overly positive narrative.

CRITICIZE – This source was recorded by his pupil, Plato, following his death. This source is an account of the trial and not the exact speech. Thus, Plato, a fellow sophist, may desire to glorify his mentor.

1. c. – Athenian democracy was not perfect in its administration of free speech. The correct answer comes straight from the document analyze.

2. d. – Socrates, Plato and Aristotle are the famous sophists from this era while Ashoka was an Indian emperor from this period.

3. a. – The effect of Alexander the Great was the spreading of the Hellenistic Culture which includes the sophists. The Polis Age recognizes an era prior to Alexander the Great. The Punic Wars marked a turning point in the Roman Republic. The Warring Period refers to an era in Chinese History at a similar period in history.

Document analysis for Questions 4–5.

SUMMARIZE – The image of Tenochtitlan shows an overhead shot of the Aztec capital. The city appears to be in the middle of a large body of water. The entire island city appears to be developed, including a large central square and streets on a grid pattern.

ANALYZE – The image supports the reputation of Tenochtitlan as a thriving urban capital. Since the city was at its peak in the 15th century, gridded streets and dense buildings imply advanced technology and design. Although there are no obvious defensive structures in the drawing, it is likely that the water served as a natural barrier to attackers.

CRITICIZE – This is a modern rendering of Tenochtitlan rather than a historical or contemporary image, so its accuracy is dependent upon the artist's knowledge of the original city layout. It is also possible that this artist is attempting to portray the reputed grandeur of Tenochtitlan rather than its realistic form.

4. d. – The Aztecs practiced peaceful diplomacy with other natives as supported by the lack of walls. While the city did not possess walls, the lake served as a natural defensive perimeter since the Aztecs used war to address diplomatic issues with neighboring tribes.

5. b. – Cuzco is the urban center associated with the Incan civilization. While the other locations are found in Native civilizations, they are not part of the Inca Empire.

Document analysis for Question 6.

SUMMARIZE – Mrs. Smart describes her work hours and how they impact her family life. She says that she works many hours and that her family helps to care for her children.

ANALYZE – The document supports generalizations about working conditions during the industrial revolution—long hours and difficult family life.

CRITICIZE – The title indicates that Mrs. Smart was interviewed in 1843 London as part of a government report. It is reasonable to assume that Mrs. Smart was speaking truthfully because the details of her testimony are very specific and personal. It is also interesting to note that this report focused on agricultural workers, showing they were also impacted by industrialization, as were the urban laborers.

6. b. – This is a difficult question because choices A and C seem to target the correct era, but they both specify urban factory problems. D deals with politics. B, the correct answer, addresses the role of women. During the Victorian period, women were brought in from the farm and made to be active and attentive mothers.

Document analysis for Questions 7–8.

SUMMARIZE – Jack Rakove argues that America's founding fathers only sought independence when the British Empire harshly responded to demands for rights as citizens.

ANALYZE – Jack Rakove's interpretation of America's founding fathers depicts them as men of circumstance rather than men of action. For this historian, America's founding fathers became revolutionary because of the events of 1773–74, such as taxation without representation, forcing them to take action.

CRITICIZE – This is a historian's interpretation of the motivation of the leadership of the American Revolution. Without knowing this particular author's motivations or his sources, we may assume that his view is reasonable.

7. b. – America's revolutionary leaders were driven, enlightened leaders with a desire for independence. Jack Ravoke challenges the depiction of America's founding fathers as enlightened men that studied the ideals of John Locke and demanded equality. Rather, he argues that America's founding fathers worked within the British colonial system until the British Empire's harsh actions pushed them to the point of revolution.

8. a. – Simon Bolivar was the leader of the Latin American Revolutions in Venezuela and Peru. As a conservative creole, he possessed a dual allegiance to his European ancestry and his American country making the decision to rebel complicated.

Document analysis for Questions 9–10.

SUMMARIZE – The excerpt addresses Jawaharlal Nehru's support of communism as India sought independence from Great Britain.

ANALYZE – The excerpt demonstrates the complex geopolitical environment that existed between capitalist and communist nations prior to the start of the Cold War. In this excerpt, Nehru notes the economic poverty in India will not be addressed by a capitalist economy, but rather a communist system.

CRITICIZE – This excerpt is taken from 1941 in the midst of World War II and prior to Indian Independence in 1947.

9. b. – Governments under the control of European colonizers sought independence. Even though many colonized nations sought independence in the name of self-determination after World War One, by the start of World War II, many colonies were still under the control of European powers like Great Britain. Therefore, leaders in nations, such as India, began speaking out and demanding independence.

10. a. – The Cold War caused many nations to turn against the United States and the Soviet Union as the two superpowers actively engaged in proxy wars throughout the world. Therefore, many nations, such as India, joined the non-alignment movement and refused to ally with either nation.

Document analysis for Questions 11–12.

> **SUMMARIZE** – Ellinas argues that wind power is the best solution to the urgent problem of climate change. He says that wind technology is ready and able to do the job, despite a lack of wind on Cyprus.
>
> **ANALYZE** – The document appears to be the reasoned opinion of a wind power expert.
>
> **CRITICIZE** – Ellinas is identified as "chairman of DK Wind Supply." It is possible that a wind executive is motivated by economic gain.

11. a. – Once you understand that the document deals with the nexus of climate change and economics, you can eliminate B, C, and D, because they all address political issues. Only A, the Copenhagen Summit, focused on climate change and its economic impact.

12. d. – Answer D is an example of a specialist with professional and economic ties to a particular solution, arguing for that solution. A and B are examples of experts sharing their expert opinions without any explicit economic benefits to themselves. Although a Volvo CEO (answer C) stands to benefit economically from improved MPG, he has no particular authority in the field of computer technology.

Short-Answer Questions

1. Analysis of the document prompt:

   SUMMARIZE – The map of the trade routes in the year 100 BCE demonstrates the complexity of interregional trade in the classical period. The map shows land and sea routes running between Europe, Africa, and Asia

   ANALYZE – The map illustrates the extent of interregional trade via the Eurasian Silk Road and Indian Ocean Trade Route. With the expansion of empires, roads were established for moving troops and became repurposed for trade. In addition, with the expansion of knowledge related to animal breeding and wind patterns, trade routes expanded throughout Eurasia.

   CRITICIZE – This source illustrates many routes but excluded the caravan routes of Trans-Saharan Africa and interregional trade networks in Mesoamerica.

(A) The prompt requires two effects on the economies referenced in the image above. The economic impact of interregional trade in this period include:

- Use of domesticated pack animals to move more goods
- Innovations in maritime trade to expand the network and access goods
- The spread of crops like cotton and rice
- Innovations in farming techniques

(B) The prompt requires one effect on the culture referenced in the map above. The cultural impact of interregional trade in this period include:

- Spread of religious ideas like Christianity, Hinduism, Judaism, and Buddhism

- Exposure to new ethnicities and languages leading to the acquisition of new words; particularly Greek.
- The Spread of Hellenistic ideas related to mathematics, philosophy and art.

2. Analysis of the prompt:

Although Periodization is no longer tested on the AP World History exam, the skill remains valuable to a thorough understanding of history. The process of naming a period of history requires you to identify and assess large trends, and identify evidence to support those trends. To answer this question, you must identify historical examples that defend and refute a generalization—that the urban centers of 600–1450 were "Cosmopolitan Cities." The word *cosmopolitan* denotes that these urban centers were sophisticated and worldly. Therefore, urban centers that participated in inter-regional trade and cultural exchange may be defined as cosmopolitan while urban centers that remained insular may not.

(A) The prompt requires two pieces of evidence that support urban centers being classified as "Cosmopolitan Cities". Urban centers matching this classification in this period include:

- Cordoba in Spain
- Venice in Italy
- Baghdad in the Abbasid Dynasty
- Chang'an in Tang China
- Constantinople in the Byzantine Empire
- Timbuktu in West Africa

(B) The prompt requires one piece of evidence that refutes urban centers being classified as "Cosmopolitan Cities". Urban centers matching this classification in this period include:

- London in England
- Moscovy in Russia
- Cuzco in Inca Empire
- Salzburg in Austria

3. Analysis of the document prompt:

SUMMARIZE – The drawing shows black men (presumably slaves) harvesting sugar cane. A white man in the image holds a whip and watches the workers. In the background, another white man appears to be beating a black man who is crouched on the ground.

ANALYZE – The image supports the argument that slaves were used to support the sugar-growing industry as sugar became a cash crop and production escalated. In the Age of Exploration, colonial empires enslaved Africans to advance their home economies. Cash crops dominated those economies, causing the rise of consumerism, an increase in slavery, and the spread of disease.

CRITICIZE – Since this document has no attribution, no critical analysis of the source is possible.

(A) The prompt requires one piece of evidence that explains a reason for the development of the mass production of crops in the 16th and/or 17th centuries. Possible answers include:

- Mercantilism
- Consumerism
- Columbian Exchange
- Cash Crop
- Plantation Economy

(B) The prompt requires two pieces of evidence from the 16th–18th centuries that explain an effect of this economic transformation. Possible answers include:

- Encomienda System
- Slave Trade
- Globalization
- Commercialization
- Indentured Servants
- Diversification of Food Crops
- Rise of Merchant Class

4. Analysis of the document prompts:

Document 1

SUMMARIZE – The document describes a time in retrospect when people had no ailments and life was orderly. He says the foreigners changed that.

ANALYZE – The document supports the notion that the Spanish conquistadors hurt the people of the Yucatan.

CRITICIZE – By the year 1550, the Spanish had controlled the Yucatan for more than 30 years. This interviewee was remembering a situation that hadn't existed for almost half of a century. It is possible, especially in light of the Spanish brutality the speaker must have witnessed more recently, that he is expressing more nostalgia than history.

Document 2

SUMMARIZE – The artist contrasts the awkwardness of a Comanche on and off of his horse, implying that the Comanche is only at home on the horse.

ANALYZE – The document implies that the Comanche people have always ridden horses, and that they would be nothing without the horse. It should be noted, however, that prior to the 16th century, there were no horses in the Americas.

CRITICIZE – Because Catlin is an artist, you might assume that he has a keen eye for detail. The awe inherent in his words may be genuine, given that he is likely seeing the Comanche from a traveler's perspective.

(A) Probably the best economic developments to use in this question are those associated with the Columbian Exchange. Both documents include evidence of European influence on Americans—disease and horses. The advent of Mercantilist policies in Europe helped to lead to an increase in exploration and colonization in the Western Hemisphere, as well as trade practices that brought goods to the Americas in exchange for gold.

(B) In addition to economics, religion also helped to accelerate the exchange between Europe and the New World. The Roman Catholic Church, in an effort to counter the erosion of its flock resulting from the Protestant Reformation, sent missionaries to convert new adherents among the Native Americans.

5. Analysis of the document prompts:

Document 1

SUMMARIZE – Rousseau details the reasons for his argument that women are essentially different from men, and that it is this difference that necessitates a unique education for women. He clearly believes that women are less able to reason abstractly than men.

ANALYZE – The document provides rather strong evidence of Rousseau's opposition to gender equality. For those who know Rousseau as an Enlightenment *philosophe*, his traditional view of women may be surprising.

CRITICIZE – This is an excerpt from *Emile*, one of Rousseau's seminal works. Although he was a product of the Enlightenment, Rousseau is often known as the Father of Romanticism. By 1762, he had begun to question rationalism and egalitarianism. The perspective expressed in this document is not surprising given Rousseau's other writings.

Document 2

SUMMARIZE – Wollstonecraft argues in direct opposition to Rousseau. In fact, she mentions Emile in the document itself. Her contention is that only independent and well-educated women can make good mothers.

ANALYZE – Wollstonecraft's writings get to the heart of the gender debate of the late 18th century. She is one of the author's who most persuasively argues for equality between men and women. By mentioning the role of mothers in creating good patriots,

Wollstonecraft appeals to the revolutionary spirit for support of gender equality.

CRITICIZE – The title of her work, *A Vindication of the Rights of Women*, was meant to parallel the popular revolutionary work, *Declaration of the Rights of Man*, written in 1789 and one of the foundational works of the French Revolution. By 1792, the revolution had gained momentum and was quickly building to a climax in the National Convention. Wollstonecraft undoubtedly wanted to insure a place for women in the new republic, so the timing of this work could not have been more appropriate. Of course, she had been a staunch proponent of equal education for women throughout her life, publishing several other works supporting that argument, so the timing of this document was likely not just opportunistic.

(A) Political developments leading to the debate over equal education for women may be drawn from England and France in this era. Beginning with the reign of James I, British women were given a restricted education. King James was famously opposed to educating women for fear they become too sly. Later, during the Enlightenment and French Revolution, men and women began to support equal education as a means to allowing women to achieve their fullest potential, a potential which had previously been undervalued.

(B) A social development which led to, or at least accelerated, the debate over education equality was the revolutionary empowerment of women in French society. Although their political rights were not supported, women began to play a greater role in social movements. For instance, The Mothers' March on Versailles in 1789 was begun by women and supported by the men of French society.

6. Analysis of the document prompt:

    SUMMARIZE – Tocqueville posits that the French Revolution began because the nobility, in their efforts to reform the French economy and society and to help the French poor, inadvertently inflamed the underclasses. He implies both noble intentions and ignorance of the potential impact of words on the poor.

ANALYZE – Tocqueville, a noted and skilled observer, offers an explanation of unintended consequences for the death and destruction of the French Revolution. Given what you probably already know about the revolution, Tocqueville's argument may seem interesting, but probably insufficient. It is likely that you learned about the role of the Jacobins and other reform-minded leaders of France, who often intentionally roused the ire of the poor to support their own goals. Additionally, since most of the early revolutionaries were constitutional monarchists, you could argue that their goals were not so noble as Tocqueville has implied. They wanted to take some power from the monarchy, but not really give any to the poor.

CRITICIZE – Several things within the source line are informative. The document is excerpted from a book written in 1856, 67 years after the start of the French Revolution. Even if you did not know that Tocqueville wasn't even born until 1805, you might question the accuracy of anyone's memory over 67 years. So, his skills as an observer are irrelevant and this is strictly a historical study. Additionally, you may want to consider the context surrounding Tocqueville's publication. He was probably writing amidst, or shortly after, the Revolutions of 1848, and during the time of Louis Napoleon Bonaparte's rise in France. The middle class, and very definitely anti-monarchist revolutionaries of 1848, bore little resemblance to those figures responsible for the start of the French Revolution. It is possible that Tocqueville's opinion of the earlier people and events was tainted by his observations of their more recent counterparts.

(A) Evidence to support Tocqueville's thesis might include the events of the Great Fear when rumored threats of the king's army attacking in the countryside inspired poor farmers to rise up. The farmers' revolt was so sudden and dangerous that the National Constituent Assembly needed to stop its constitutional development and at least imply a promise of tax relief to quell the storm. Notably, the farmers never rejoined the revolution and returned to their former conservative values. In this case, it appears that talk of revolution and tax reform was the driving force of the uprising.

(B) To undermine Tocqueville's argument, you could use the example of the Sans Culottes, who intentionally inflamed the urban poor to pressure the nobility for their own purposes. In this case, it was neither inadvertent aristocratic talk nor unintentional inflammation of the poor that provoked the uprisings that led to a republican government.

(C) Whereas you may be hard pressed to cite examples to support Tocqueville, you will likely have very little difficulty finding examples of revolutions that were not caused by the careless words of well-meaning aristocrats. The Russian Revolution of 1917, for instance, began as a bubbling over of dissatisfaction with the status quo. The monarchy, in its attempt to brutally suppress disgruntled workers in St. Petersburg, inspired even more revolutionary sentiment and quickly lost control of the situation. Any number of the anti-imperialist revolts of the 20th century might also be used as evidence against Tocqueville's point.

7. Analysis of the prompt:

   For a compare and contrast Short-Answer Question, you're required to identify historical examples that demonstrate similarities and differences between historical eras. In this comparison SAQ, you must compare and contrast different totalitarian leaders as well as account for a historical development that caused a shift in policy.

(A) The prompt requires one piece of evidence that denotes a similarity between absolute and fascist leaders. Similarities include:

- Command Economy
- Militarism
- Colonialism
- Racist Doctrine
- Manipulation of the Arts
- Caste System
- Use of Violence

(B) The prompt requires one piece of evidence that denotes a difference between absolute and fascist leaders. Differences include:

- Views on Religion
- Bureaucratic Elite
- Social Darwinism
- Nationalism
- Disdain of Communism

(C) The prompt requires one piece of evidence that explains a historical reason for the difference between the policies of absolute and fascist leaders. Possible historical developments include:

- New Modes of Communication like the Radio
- New Modes of Transportation like the Steam Boat and/or Airplane
- Implications of World War I
- Shifts in the Balance of Power
- Impact of the Great Depression

8. Analysis of the document prompts:

Document 1

SUMMARIZE – The document details conditions under which boys worked at a particular factory. It suggests that the working conditions are so horrible they seem unbelievable, but that they are true.

ANALYZE – Here is explicit evidence of at least one factory that has taken advantage of its workers—specifically young boys who are forced to work more than 48 hours straight. It can be used to substantiate the underside of industrialization.

CRITICIZE – This document is excerpted from a factory inspector's report. We have no way to know if the inspector had a particular agenda for his report—for instance, to expose abuses or to cover up abuses. Because the report was presented to Parliament, however, it may be that the inspector attempted to be as detailed and accurate as possible to demonstrate his value in the eyes of the government.

Document 2

SUMMARIZE – This is a photograph of a man and a boy standing among the machines of a factory. The man is looking down at the boy, who appears to be staring at the machines in front of them. There seem to be many machines in this factory, but it is impossible to count them in this image.

ANALYZE – The document provides a firsthand, albeit momentary, look inside a factory. It also seems to support the contention that children were hired routinely because it appears as though the man is instructing the boy.

CRITICIZE – The citation on this document states only that it is a photograph from 1903. Without any other information, we have no way of knowing the photographer's intentions.

(A) The Second Industrial Revolution introduced mechanized industry to Europe. Because urban factories lacked a ready workforce, it was necessary that the factory owners hire women and children. As an added bonus, these groups of laborers tended to work for much lower wages than their male counterparts.

(B) As a result of child labor and the imposition of extremely long hours, eventually Parliament expanded regulations designed to restrict the power and independence of factory owners and provide greater union support for workers. Finally, in 1906, the Labour Party was formed.

(C) Similar conditions existed in Germany, where industrial production nearly doubled in the closing decades of the 19th century. There Bismarck supported better working conditions to insure the health and wellbeing of the German workers. Although he supported a healthier workforce, however, Bismarck did not support shorter hours. He, like the business owners in Germany, believed in the overwhelming benefit of hard work.

9. Analysis of the document prompt:

SUMMARIZE – Subtelny details some of the horrors of the Great Purge of 1937 in Ukraine. He lists the many Ukrainian groups that were eliminated in mass executions which may have numbered in the hundreds of thousands.

ANALYZE – The evidence presented in this document is important to our understanding of the brutality of the Soviet regime under Stalin. Additionally, it lends credence to the argument that Ukrainians were victims of one of the greatest mass murders in history.

CRITICIZE – All we know from the source line is the author, title, and date of publication. In this case, the information gives us very little on which we might base our assessments.

(A) The Great Purge was the result of Stalin's attempt to eliminate all political opposition, and, in the case of Ukraine, gain complete control over the "breadbasket of Eastern Europe." His ruthlessness led to the murder of hundreds of thousands.

(B) The impact of the purge on the Ukrainian mentality is beyond description. But one specific effect was that the Ukrainians welcomed the Nazi army when it invaded in 1941. After losing so many to the Stalinist purge, the Ukrainians saw the Nazis as saviors. Of course, thousands more died at the hands of the Nazis in the winter of 1941-42. As a further insult, the Ukrainians were labeled Nazi collaborators at the end of the war, a label that persists in some circles even today.

(C) Perhaps the simplest parallel is France during the Terror. Just like Stalin, the leaders of the Committee of Public Safety targeted thousands of political opponents for execution.

10. Analysis of the document prompt:

SUMMARIZE – Reitan outlines Margaret Thatcher's successful campaign to restrict immigration to the UK from its Commonwealth territories. He suggests that she managed this feat by appealing to the basically racist sentiments of both Conservatives and Labour, who each supported the Nationality Act of 1981 for their own anti-immigrant reasons.

ANALYZE – The document is important evidence to support the strength of Thatcher's leadership as illustrated by her ability to identify common ground and cobble together the necessary votes to push through her own agenda. Reitan also provides some persuasive points to support his contention that the Thatcher years were driven by nationalism and racism.

CRITICIZE – Since this 2002 study sees the Thatcher years as "revolutionary," Reitan might be expected to overstate the impact of Thatcher herself and understate the influence of historical context. It seems, however, based on this brief excerpt, that this is not the case.

(A) This part of your answer might be based entirely on the document. The fact that the bill targets only Commonwealth immigrants—those immigrants coming from former British colonies—implies a connection with ethnic makeup. Whereas Irish, Scottish, and Welsh immigrants to Britain had always enjoyed free passage, and EU members continued to enjoy the same, immigrants from places like India were denied citizenship according to this new law.

(B) Despite the argument in Part A, you might also cite evidence from the 1990s that points to a series of new laws that restricted immigrants from Eastern Europe. As the Soviet Union and its partners crumbled, the flow of refugees from the eastern part of the continent to the UK increased dramatically. In response, Parliament passed a series of laws aimed at restricting that flow. Because these restrictions were aimed at other Europeans—ethnically similar to the British—you could argue that the Nationality Act of 1981 was just the first in a series of Conservative laws limiting all immigration to the UK.

(C) A very recent example would be Hungary's response to a flood of Syrian immigrants in 2015. The Hungarian government erected fences and posted soldiers along the border to prevent these new immigrants from entering. Similarly, Hungary and others who tried to stem the flow of these new refugees were accused of racist motives.

Source Credits

About the Author

Tony Maccarella teaches social studies, including AP World History and AP Macroeconomics, at Saddle River Day School in Saddle River, New Jersey. He has been teaching since 1982, and in addition to AP European History, he has also taught AP U.S. History, Comparative Governments, Anthropology, Psychology, and Military History.

Since 2002, Tony has served as a Reader and Table Leader for the AP European History exam. He is responsible for scoring AP European History exam questions, supervising other readers, and assisting with the clarification of scoring standards.

SHERPALEARNING

GUIDING YOU TO EVEN GREATER HEIGHTS

www.sherpalearning.com

Made in the USA
Las Vegas, NV
28 November 2022

60571294R00125